10TH YEAR ANN

Talit ha Cumi

The SECRETS OF THE PRAYER SHAWL

JOHN FRANCIS

This book is dedicated to:

❖ My wife, Penny, whose depth and wealth of knowledge never ceases to amaze me

❖ Prophetess Juanita Bynum, who gave me my first tallit

❖ Rabbi James, for valuable insight into the Jewish religion and practices

❖ Angela Shears & Dr Mohammed Johnson, thank you for all of your help in making this book possible

It is my pleasure and honour to present to you this special

NEW EDITION of Talitha Cumi

Celebrating 10 Years of the Release of Talitha Cumi

Additional Resources by Bishop John Francis

BOOKS

Walking in Your Assignment: Finding Your Purpose & Destiny

Is There a Word from the Lord?

What Do You Do When You're Left Alone?

10 Steps to Get out of Debt

The Pastors & Church Workers Handbook

CDs

Finally, Bishop John Francis

One Lord, One Faith

Manifestation of the Promise

Welcome in this Place

Talitha Cumi

Secrets of the Prayer Shawl

John Francis

Copyright © 2007 First Edition, Second Edition 2017 Bishop John Francis
www.johnfrancis.org.uk
Published by Sekal Publishing
all rights reserved.

Print ISBN: 978-0-9957999-0-5
EBook ISBN: 978-0-9957999-1-2

For Worldwide Distribution, Printed in Great Britain

Contents

Author's Personal Note

It would be wrong of me to begin the second edition of this book without again mentioning briefly where my initial interest in prayer was created. I grew up in a Christian home where regular prayer was a normal part of my daily life and routine. My father, the late Bishop T.G. Francis, instilled in me the importance of a regular prayer life. As a young boy, I never fully understood or welcomed the 6 a.m. prayer sessions that we as a family were expected to attend in our living room each morning. There were no exceptions to this rule, and I would have happily swapped an hour or two on my knees for my warm bed and pillow any day!

Now that I am older, I am glad that my father took the time to introduce me to prayer at such a young age. I can honestly say that there have been so many occasions in my life when I have been so grateful to have the foundation of prayer to rely on in my Christian walk.

There truly is power in prayer; and as each season of my life passes, I find that I rely on prayer as an integral part of my life more and more. I know that if it were not for prayer I would not be alive today. My mother was diagnosed with cancer before I was born. My parents had been told by the doctors that my mother had an inoperable brain tumor and that she didn't have much longer to live. They had concluded that there was nothing they could do for her, and had actually sent her home to die. The only help the doctors were able to provide was some pain relief medication.

My father wasn't prepared to accept this fate for her and continued to pray for her healing. If the doctors couldn't do anything, then he was sure that his God could! He didn't believe it was God's will that my mother should die.

After much prayer and my father's obedience to God's Word, my mother was healed of cancer. I was born after my mother was healed, although the doctors advised my father that having more children could result in her death. My father believed that if God had allowed my mother to become pregnant, then He would keep her through the pregnancy.

My mother, Elfreda Francis, defying the odds, not only gave birth to my sister, but became pregnant again and gave birth to me. My mother is still alive today—a living testimony to the power of prayer. I have seen the lives of many changed in remarkable ways because prayer was seen as a real and tangible solution to their impossible situation.

A few years ago, I spoke on the topic of *Talitha Cumi* at a conference called Praise Power. As I was preaching, I felt led of the Lord to place the tallit I was using on a lady in the congregation who was confined to a wheelchair. She immediately got up out of the wheelchair and started worshipping God. I later found out that she had been completely healed of cancer that evening; and when I visited the same conference a year later, she was still rejoicing, still completely healed, and she no longer needed the wheelchair.

Prayer is powerful and wonderful, and my desire is that all will discover the joy, strength, and peace that a dedicated life of prayer can bring.

Preface

My journey begins with the growing popularity within the Christian community of a large piece of tapestry cloth measuring approximately six feet in length by four feet. I become intrigued by this sacred garment that has its roots in the Jewish community. As time passed, I became more curious about this piece of cloth and its association with prayer.

To be honest, when I was given my first prayer shawl, I wasn't really sure what I should do with it. I wanted to use the prayer shawl in the right way and at the right time. I had so many questions: Why was this beautifully embroidered piece of tapestry so closely linked with prayer? What, if any, was its significance or link with the Bible? Is it still relevant today? How should it be used? When should it be used? Was I, being non-Jewish—a Gentile—allowed to use it?

Its significant link to the Word of God and to prayer became real to me in a new way after hearing my wife, Penny, teach and preach about the prayer shawl—the *tallit*—during our annual Prophetic, Prayer, and Praise Conference.

After hearing my wife's teaching, I realized how strategic certain Scriptures are. Although they seemed unrelated, they were in fact divinely linked by God. My questions were answered; it was amazing! Our family had lived in a Jewish community for several years, and I was now seeing my neighbors with new, enlightened eyes. Through a piece of cloth, God had revealed an ancient truth that revolutionized my prayer life.

The first edition of this book was released in 2007 and not only changed my life, but thousands of others as well. This expanded edition delves much more deeply into prayer, some Jewish traditions that the Lord gave His people, and the gifts of prayer and praise we can offer to our heavenly Father today.

I hope and pray you are touched by His mighty love and grace today and every day.

Bishop John Francis

Introduction

Revolutionize your prayer life by discovering ancient biblical truths combined with today's revelations!

Then the Lord said to Moses, "Give the following instructions to the people of Israel: Throughout the generations to come you must **make tassels for the hems of your clothing and attach them with a blue cord. When you see the tassels, you will remember and obey all the commands of the Lord** instead of following your own desires and defiling yourselves, as you are prone to do. The tassels will help you remember that you must obey all my commands and be holy to your God (Numbers 15:37-40).

In this new, exciting, and expanded edition of the best-selling *Talitha Cumi,* you will learn secrets of life-changing magnitude! Bishop John Francis takes you to overlooked passages in God's Word—key Scriptures that link the prayer shawl—the tallit—with the power of God.

You will discover:

- The tallit's significant role in prayer
- Why and how the tallit is made

- The significance of the tassels
- Why the color blue is important
- How to wear your tallit as a sanctuary
- How to become more intimate with God
- How to restore the sacredness of your prayer time
- And much more!

This exceptional book brings an ancient custom—and command—into your modern-day spiritual experience in a whole new way. Combining relevant Scripture with up-to-date and meaningful personal and worldwide knowledge, your Christian journey will be enhanced, taken to a higher level.

Bishop Francis is the founder and senior pastor of Ruach City Church—one church in several locations in London and in Philadelphia, PA, USA. He is a multitalented and multifaceted man of God; not only a prolific writer but also presents: a television broadcast, *Order My Steps*, with 126 million worldwide viewers; oversees 50 churches in the UK and overseas; recently launched Ruach Radio; He is the founder of The Inspirational Choir (UK); and was awarded the Minister of the Year Oasis Award. Bishop Francis's wife, Penny, is the Co-Pastor of Ruach City Church and has worked alongside him throughout his ministry. They have three lovely daughters.

Chapter 1
The Tallit: The Word

Then He [Jesus] came to the house of the ruler of the synagogue, and saw a tumult and those who wept and wailed loudly. When He came in, He said to them, "Why make this commotion and weep? The child is not dead, but sleeping." And they ridiculed Him. But when He had put them all outside, He took the father and the mother of the child, and those who were with Him, and entered where the child was lying. Then **He took the child by the hand, and said to her, "Talitha, cumi,"** **which is translated, "[Damsel], I say to you, arise."** **Immediately the girl arose and walked,** for she was twelve years of age. And they were overcome with great amazement (Mark 5:35-36,38-42 NKJV).

Inside that room a miraculous event took place centered on two words, *"Talitha, cumi"* and the touch of the hand of Jesus. When Jesus spoke those words while holding her hand, the young girl was brought back to life. Her parents were overjoyed. Life had been restored to their beloved daughter.

There is a deeper meaning for the words Jesus uttered that day. It is probable that this young girl was lying on her deathbed covered in a *tallit* or wrapped in a tallit as a burial shroud, symbolizing that she was under the hand of the Almighty and subject to His tender mercies.

Jairus, her father, was a synagogue official and understood the significance of the tallit (pronounced tah-leet) and the tzitzit (pronounced tsee-tseet). He knew the promises of God bring health and healing to those who adhere to His commandments and devote their lives to Him. Jairus had heard Jesus teach and knew that He was the very son of God. He knew that there was healing in the name of Jesus, and that He was capable of miracles.

It should be noted that in translation, *talitha* is also associated with the words "lamb" and "covering,"[1] which give us an even more revelatory understanding of the words Talitha, cumi: Young woman (who is covered by the tallit), airse.[2] Such a statement would surely have been marveled at by the girl's parents and warranted Jesus' stipulation of secrecy, especially as the New Testament Scriptures record only three canonical instances where Jesus raised the dead (the young girl in Matthew 9:25; the young boy in Luke 7:14; Lazarus in John 11:43-44). And, of course, being God, He raised Himself from the dead.

In making that statement and affirming it with the miracle, Jesus had declared His deity (He is God in the flesh) to all present—a fact He did not want to become public knowledge, as His time had not yet come. *"Jesus gave them strict orders not to tell anyone what had happened, and then he told them to give her something to eat"* (Mark 5:43).

Looking further into the spiritual significance of this miracle, we can consider that the girl was wrapped in a *tallit with tzitzit* (representing the commandments of God or the Word of God) and that Jesus as the Lamb of God, was her covering—the Word become flesh.

> *In the beginning the Word [Jesus] already existed. The Word was with God, and the Word was God (John 1:1).*

> So the Word [Jesus] became human and made his home among us. He was full of unfailing love and faithfulness. And we have seen his glory, the glory of the Father's one and only Son (John 1:14).

The scene presented with the young girl is itself unique: Jesus, the manifested Word of God, raises the daughter of Jairus, who is wrapped up in the Word. This is a truth that we as believers should grasp hold of—when God is presented with His Word, He can do nothing else but be moved by it and fulfill it.

Let's be wrapped up in the Word.

As part of the usual Jewish practice in the circumstances of death, it is customary for a Jewish male to be buried with his tallit wrapped around him. It is also customary for a female corpse to be covered with a tallit while being prepared for burial.

The girl was wrapped in a physical cloth, a tallit, and in a spiritual cloth of prayer and belief in the great Healer. Not only did Jairus seek God through Jesus for healing for his daughter, but the family and community members were praying as well. Prayer always grabs the attention of the Almighty.

"Talitha, cumi"

Let's look more closely at what Jesus spoke as He grasped the young girl's hand. *"Talitha, cumi"* is an Aramaic phrase and generally interpreted as "'Damsel,' 'Daughter,' or 'Little girl,' I say to you, arise."[3] However, several experts in this field tend to agree that there is more meant by these two words than has been initially interpreted. Jesus was speaking to her spirit, which affected her physical body.

Because we know she was twelve years old and under Jewish law considered a woman, the emphasis in translation would not be little girl as most of the modern-day Bible versions interpret this phrase. Scholars have suggested that if Jesus had said and meant, "Young girl, arise," He would have used the Aramaic word *talya* and the possibly absolute form, *talyatha,* not *talitha.* The Aramaic absolute form of tallit is *tallitha*. Further investigation also suggests that if Jesus had meant to say "Damsel, arise," He would have said *Talyatha, qumi*, not *Talitha, cumi.*[4]

In all translations, the age of the young girl is consistent; she was twelve years of age. Age in years is concrete, but age in other terms is relative to cultures and traditions of the society. Whether considered a damsel, little girl, young woman, or child, this precious daughter of distraught parents was brought back to life by the living God through His Son Jesus.

***

The same day that the girl was raised from the dead, Jesus had healed the woman who had been bleeding for twelve years.

> *As Jesus was saying this, the leader of a synagogue came and knelt before him. **"My daughter has just died," he said, "but you can bring her back to life again if you just come and lay your hand on her." So Jesus and his disciples got up and went with him.** Just then a **woman who had suffered for twelve years with constant bleeding came up behind him. She touched the fringe of his robe, for she thought, "If I can just touch his robe, I will be healed"** (Matthew 9:18-21).*

Then a leader of the local synagogue, whose name was Jairus, arrived. When he saw Jesus, he fell at his feet, pleading fervently with him. **"My little daughter is dying,"** he said. **"Please come and lay your hands on her; heal her so she can live."** **Jesus went with him,** and all the people followed, crowding around him. A woman in the crowd had suffered for twelve years with constant bleeding. She had suffered a great deal from many doctors, and over the years she had spent everything she had to pay them, but she had gotten no better. In fact, she had gotten worse. **She had heard about Jesus, so she came up behind him through the crowd and touched his robe. For she thought to herself, "If I can just touch his robe, I will be healed"** (Mark 5:22-28).

> ***Then a man named Jairus,*** *a leader of the local synagogue, came and **fell at Jesus' feet,** pleading with him to come home with him. **His only daughter, who was about twelve years old, was dying.** As **Jesus went with him,** he was surrounded by the crowds. **A woman in the crowd** had suffered for twelve years with constant bleeding, and she could find no cure. Coming up behind Jesus, she **touched the fringe of his robe. Immediately, the bleeding stopped*** (Luke 8:41-44).

We realize from reading Scripture that before the young girl was brought back to life, a woman with a rare illness was healed—just by touching Jesus' robe.

The Bible is not a book of coincidences.

It is important to realize that the Bible is not a book of coincidences or accidents. Every word is divinely inspired by God. Therefore, it is generally accepted that throughout the Bible details are given that purposefully aim to guide each reader to a specific truth.

One thing in particular that drew my attention was the fact that the woman with the issue of blood had suffered for twelve years—and Jairus' daughter was twelve years old (Mark 5:42; Luke 8:42). This suggested to me that these two events were divinely linked for some reason and that there was definitely more to each story.

After the woman is healed, Jesus continues on His journey with Jairus but is interrupted by a servant from Jairus' house informing him that there is no need for Jesus to come; his daughter had died.

> *While he [Jesus] was still speaking to her, messengers arrived from the home of Jairus, the leader of the synagogue. They told him, "**Your daughter is dead.** There's no use troubling the Teacher now." But **Jesus overheard them and***

said to Jairus, "Don't be afraid. Just have faith"
(Mark 5:35-36).

Jesus admonishes Jairus not to fear but to believe, and they continue on their journey to his house. On arrival at the house Jesus makes a point of removing all the mourners and the general family members from the room, allowing only Peter, James, John, her mother and father to enter (Mark 5:37).

At this point we see where the healing of the woman with the issue of blood becomes significant. The key is connected to the action of touching. To understand the significance of the touching that is taking place, we need to first understand a particular aspect of Jewish Law. According to the Law, one could become ritually unclean simply by touching or coming into contact with someone or something unclean. The Law specified that a woman experiencing bleeding was considered unclean, and the dead were considered unclean.

> *If a woman has a **flow of blood** for many days that is unrelated to her menstrual period, or if the blood continues beyond the normal period, **she is ceremonially unclean.** As during her menstrual period, **the woman will be unclean** as long as the discharge continues (Leviticus 15:25).*

> **All those who touch a dead human body** *will be ceremonially* **unclean** *for seven days* (Numbers 19:11).

Therefore, from the perspective of the Law, this woman should not have been among the crowds surrounding Jesus, as everyone who came into contact with her would also be considered unclean.

From the following Scripture passages, we can see that when she is questioned by Jesus, she is clearly embarrassed and ashamed as she declares that she has indeed broken the Law.

> **Immediately the bleeding stopped,** *and she could feel in her body that she had been healed of her terrible condition.* **Jesus realized at once that healing power had gone out from him, so he turned around in the crowd and asked, "Who touched my robe?"** *His disciples said to him, "Look at this crowd pressing around you. How can you ask, 'Who touched me?'"* *But he kept on looking around to see who had done it.* **Then the frightened woman, trembling at the realization of what had happened to her, came and fell to her knees in front of him and told him what she had done.** *And he said to her, "Daughter, your faith has made you well. Go in peace. Your suffering is over"* (Mark 5:29-34).

"Who touched me?" Jesus asked. Everyone denied it, and Peter said, "Master, this whole crowd is pressing up against you." But **Jesus said, "Someone deliberately touched me, for I felt healing power go out from me."** When the woman realized that she could not stay hidden, **she began to tremble and fell to her knees in front of him. The whole crowd heard her explain why she had touched him and that she had been immediately healed** (Luke 8:45-47).

When this woman touched the hem of Jesus' garment, He would have been deemed unclean in the eyes of the Law. This is important to note, as Jesus later enters the room of the dead girl—also considered unclean— and takes hold of her hand. A rabbi would not normally do this, as such an action would render him unclean. This issue of cleanliness and uncleanliness was trumped in response to faith—the woman's faith had healed her and the faith of the girl's father brought the youngster back to life.

Faith heals.

A series of events flow together to culminate in two compassion acts of healing—changing the lives of two, but impacting hundreds of relatives and onlookers. As Jesus is on His way to heal the young girl, He is interrupted by the woman with the issue of blood. During the delay, the little girl dies, so Jesus is no longer expected to heal her but to raise her from the dead. Because people would marvel and realize the power of God more if a girl was raised from the dead than one healed from sickness, perhaps God had divinely ordered the events to bring Him the greater glory.

Does this experience bring to mind another time when Jesus' delay caused concern and then marvel?

> *So the two sisters sent a message to Jesus telling him, **"Lord, your dear friend is very sick."** But when Jesus hears about it he said, "Lazarus's sickness will not end in death. No, **it happened for the glory of God so that the Son of God will receive glory** from this." ... When Jesus arrived at Bethany, he was told that **Lazarus had already been in his grave for four days.** Bethany was only a few miles down the road from Jerusalem, and many of the people had come to console Martha and Mary in their loss. ... Jesus was still angry as he arrived at the tomb, a cave with a stone rolled across its entrance. "Roll the stone aside," Jesus told them. But Martha, the dead man's sister, protested, "Lord, he has been dead for four days. The smell will be terrible."*

Jesus responded, "Didn't I tell you that you would see God's glory if you believe?" So they rolled the stone aside. Then Jesus looked up to heaven and said, "Father, thank you for hearing me. You always hear me, but I said it out loud for the sake of all these people standing here, so that they will believe you sent me." Then Jesus shouted, "Lazarus, come out!" And the dead man came out, his hands and feet bound in graveclothes, his face wrapped in a headcloth. Jesus told them, "Unwrap him and let him go!" (John 11:3-4, 17-19, 38-44).

God's plan is the best plan—no matter who is involved and what we think the timing should be. Mary and Martha, Lazarus' sisters were distraught that their brother was ill—and devastated that Jesus didn't arrive sooner to save Lazarus from dying. Yet, they knew that God through Jesus works all things for good and for His glory, according to His plan (see Ephesians 1:11). This is what we need to remember when facing problems that seem deadly.

God works all things for good and His glory.

It is logical to consider that Lazarus would have been wrapped in his tallit, therefore he was covered, even surrounded, in prayer. The prayers of the righteous are powerful and when Jesus saw the crowd gathered, just as He saw the people at Jairus' house, mourning the death of their loved one, He wept as well (John 11:35).

Did Jesus weep for a friend who died or did He weep for the curse of dying, that any of God's children have to die. Death was one of the consequences of the Fall—when Adam and Eve chose to disobey God.

> *Then the Lord God said, "Look, the human beings have become like us, knowing both good and evil.* **What if they reach out, take fruit from the tree of life, and eat it? Then they will live forever!"** *So the Lord God banished them from the Garden of Eden, and he sent Adam out to cultivate the ground from which he had been made. After sending them out, the Lord God stationed mighty cherubim to the east of the Garden of Eden. And* **he placed a flaming sword that flashed back and forth to guard the way to the tree of life** (Genesis 3:22-24).

From then on, humankind has been subject to physical death. Although our Creator provided us amazing bodies that can regenerate skin cells and recover from serious injury, our earthly bodies are frail and fragile and subject to disease and illness. Body parts wear out and our minds deteriorate. Our bones become brittle and our muscles soften. But those of us who believe have a new body to look forward to inhabiting.

Paul wrote to the believers in Corinth about sin and death:

> *Then, when our dying bodies have been transformed into bodies that will never die, this Scripture will be fulfilled: "Death is swallowed up in victory. O death, where is your victory? O death, where is your sting?" For sin is the sting that results in death, and the law gives sin its power.* **But thank God! He gives us victory over sin and death through our Lord Jesus Christ** (1 Corinthians 15:54-57).

When Jesus, the Word speaks, whether it be "Damsel, arise," or "Who touched Me?" or "Lazarus, come out!" we are assured that healing and life are speaking. His Word is not only for those who lived back in biblical days; no, His Word is alive and well with us today—every day.

Each time we delve in the Bible, we are taking another step closer to Jesus. From Genesis to Revelation, the Word of God uniquely touches everyone who reads it. When you allow the Holy Spirit to open your spiritual eyes and ears, heart and mind, a new life of prayer awaits you. You will be drawn to your heavenly Father as never before.

Prayer

Father God, we thank You for Your unfathomable blessings and are grateful for Your mercy and grace.

We praise You and lift up the name of Your Son, Jesus, as He was willing to make the ultimate sacrifice for us, so we can live forever in Your presence. May Your loving arms enfold us as a tallit, a prayer shawl, that You spoke of in Numbers and Deuteronomy that reminds us of Your commandments. Lord God, we wish to please You by being obedient to You. Give us the power and the strength to live for You daily. In Jesus' precious name, amen.

Chapter 2
What Is a Tallit?

Then the Lord said to Moses, "Give the following instructions to the people of Israel: Throughout the generations to come you must make tassels for the hems of your clothing and attach them with a blue cord. When you see the tassels, you will remember and obey all the commands of the Lord instead of following your own desires and defiling yourselves, as you are prone to do. The tassels will help you remember that you must obey all my commands and be holy to your God (Numbers 15:37-40).

You must put four tassels on the hem of the cloak with which you cover yourself—on the front, back, and sides (Deuteronomy 22:12).

Would you be surprised to learn that the death of one person prompted Almighty God to bring into effect a commandment that would affect millions of lives for thousands of years?

Would you be amazed to know that God loves His people so much that He considered losing one person to sin, is one too many?

If someone told you that God had designed a way to help His people to never sin again so that He wouldn't have to punish them, wouldn't you want to know what it is?

If your answer is yes, then read on, because spiritual revelation continues to unfold in the following pages of this book that will radically change your life.

God designed a way...

We begin with the story of a Hebrew man who went out on the Sabbath day to gather some sticks. We presume he needed the sticks to make a fire. At the time he was gathering the sticks, he never imagined that his simple act would cost him his life. It wasn't the fact that he was gathering the sticks that was the problem. The problem was his timing.

God had given commandments to His people, and they had promised to adhere to them. According to the Torah,[1] God gave 613 commandments to His people.[2] Most people tend to concentrate on only the first ten of these commandments.

> Then the Lord said to Moses, **"Write down all these instructions, for they represent the terms of the covenant I am making with you and with Israel."** Moses remained there on the mountain with the Lord forty days and forty nights. In all that time he ate no bread and

drank no water. And the Lord wrote the terms of the covenant—the Ten Commandments—on the stone tablets (Exodus 34:27-28).

He [God] proclaimed his covenant—the Ten Commandments—which he commanded you to keep, *and which he wrote on two stone tablets. It was at that time that the Lord commanded me to teach you his decrees and regulations so you would obey them in the land you are about to enter and occupy* (Deuteronomy 4:13-14).

You must not have any other god but me.
You must not make for yourself an idol of any kind or an image of anything in the heavens or on the earth or in the sea.
You must not misuse the name of the Lord your God. The Lord will not let you go unpunished if you misuse his name.
Remember to observe the Sabbath day by keeping it holy.
Honor your father and mother. Then you will live a long, full life in the land the Lord your God is giving you.
You must not murder.
You must not commit adultery.
You must not steal.
You must not testify falsely against your neighbor.

You must not covet your neighbor's house.
You must not covet your neighbor's wife,
male or female servant, ox or donkey, or
anything else that belongs to your neighbor
(Exodus 20:3-4,7-8,12-17).

When God gave His commandments to Moses, He made it clear that He had entered into covenant with Israel and that His people were to learn these laws and follow them.

On the day that this man went to gather sticks, he broke one of God's commandments. God had given a commandment to His people that they were to do no work on *Shabbat* (the Sabbath) and that they were to remember the Shabbat and keep it holy for Him.

People tend to get caught up with one particular day of the week, but careful study has shown that in the Bible, Shabbat is represented by a certain day of the week and times and seasons in the year. The word "Shabbat" simply means rest or repose, a time to set aside for God and His service. God's people were instructed to remember His feasts and holy days and keep them sacred.

I am about to build a Temple to honor the name
*of the Lord my God. It will be **a place set apart***
to burn fragrant incense before him, to display
the special sacrificial bread, and to sacrifice

burnt offerings each morning and evening, on the Sabbaths, *at new moon celebrations, and at the other appointed festivals of the Lord our God.* ***He has commanded Israel to do these things forever*** (2 Chronicles 2:4).

God had entered into a covenant—a relationship with promise—with His people. God had promised to bless them and their children and their children's children. He had promised to provide for them, make them rich and prosperous, and protect them as long as they were obedient to His commandments or laws.

If you ***fully obey the Lord your God and carefully keep all his commands*** *that I am giving you today, the Lord your God will set you high above all the nations of the world.* ***You will experience all these blessings if you obey the Lord your God:***

Your towns and your fields will be blessed. Your children and your crops will be blessed. The offspring of your ***herds and flocks will be blessed.*** *Your fruit baskets and breadboards will be blessed.* ***Wherever you go and whatever you do, you will be blessed.***

The Lord will conquer your enemies *when they attack you. They will attack you from one direction, but they will scatter from you in seven! The Lord will* ***guarantee a blessing on***

everything you do and will fill your storehouses with grain. The Lord your God will **bless you in the land** he is giving you.

If you obey the commands of the Lord your God and walk in his ways, the Lord will **establish you as his holy people** as he swore he would do. Then all the nations of the world will see that you are a people claimed by the Lord, and they will stand in awe of you.

The Lord will give you **prosperity** in the land he swore to your ancestors to give you, blessing you with **many children, numerous livestock, and abundant crops.** The Lord will send **rain** at the proper time from his rich treasury in the heavens and will bless all the work you do. You will lend to many nations, but you will **never need to borrow** from them.

If you listen to these commands of the Lord your God that I am giving you today, and if you carefully obey them, **the Lord will make you the head and not the tail, and you will always be on top and never at the bottom.** You must not turn away from any of the commands I am giving you today, nor follow after other gods and worship them (Deuteronomy 28:1-14).

This passage of Scripture makes God's intentions really

simple: those who obey Him would receive every benefit, as long as they were a holy people faithful to God.

But this poor man broke the commandment about the Sabbath (Shabbat); he had sinned. It could have been any one of the commandments, but on this occasion, he broke the one regarding the Shabbat. It is clear from the following verses that the people didn't know what to do with him. The consequences of his sin were severe—death by stoning.

> The people who found him doing this took him before Moses, Aaron, and the rest of the community. **They held him in custody because they did not know what to do with him.** Then the Lord said to Moses, "The man must be put to death! The whole community must stone him outside the camp." So the whole community took the man outside the camp and stoned him to death, just as the Lord had commanded Moses (Numbers 15:33-36).

One man's death was enough—was one too many. Therefore, God immediately gave Moses instructions about customizing their garments so as not to forget His commandments, *"Then the Lord said to Moses, 'Give the following instructions to the people of Israel: Throughout the generations to come you must make tassels for the hems of your clothing and attach them with a blue cord'"* (Numbers 15:37-38).

One man's fatal mistake moved God quickly into action. He told Moses to tell the people to put fringes on the hems of their garments, and the fringes should be attached with a blue cord. God explained that He wanted His people to do this so they could look at the fringes with blue and remember the commandments that God had given them and keep them. He wanted His people to remember His laws and obey them. Our compassionate God didn't want anyone else to die.

God desires no one to perish.

Every time they wore their garments, which roughly resembled cloaks, they would see the fringes with blue and remember. Every time they washed their garments, they would remember. Wherever, whenever, or whatever— they would always remember the commandments of the Lord. They would be wrapped up in his Word, the *tallit* (pronounced tal-EET).

Originally, the word "tallit" (also spelled *tallis*) meant cloak or mantle, a sort of blanket or shawl that men wore around their shoulders as they went about their daily lives in ancient times. At the four corners of this cloak, fringes were attached in accordance with the biblical commandment cited in Numbers 15:38-41.

A Prayer Shawl

After the Israelites were exiled from the land of Israel, as a result of being dispersed to different lands, they began to dress according to the fashion of the Gentiles around them. The tallit was no longer worn as a daily cloak; it became a religious garment—a prayer shawl—worn only at prayer time, at home, or in the synagogue. The synagogue is a building used for Jewish worship services, prayer, and study. It replaced the ancient temple or tabernacle of God's people.

The tallit is an authentic Jewish garment. Put simply, it is a rectangular-shaped garment with parallel stripes across the shorter ends. Most *tallitot* (plural of tallit) are white with navy or black stripes. It is important to note that it was originally woven without seams.

The tallit has fringes called *tzitzit* attached to each of its four corners, each having a cord of blue. It has a neckband called *atarah*, which contains the Hebrew prayer recited before donning the garment. The garment can be made of only one of the following fabrics: linen, wool, silk, or synthetic material (polyester). The fabric of a tallit worn by a Levite should not be mixed.[3]

Wearing the tallit is a Jewish spiritual practice derived from a verse in the Torah (the first five books of the Hebrew Scriptures), in Numbers 15. The tallit is popularly known as a prayer shawl. In traditional Judaism, the rabbis describe the Torah as "the garment of the soul," and the tallit is used to protect the scrolls of the Torah when they are moved.

An old tallit that is unsightly, torn, or unusable is donated to the synagogue or a Judaic library. It is then used to wrap worn or superfluous documents, such as photocopies, that include the name YHVH *(Adonai),* the sacred name of God in Hebrew script, for burial with dignity in a *geniza,* Hebrew for "hiding place."[4]

The tallit is a cloak that envelopes a person physically and spiritually in prayer and celebration and in joy and sorrow.

Although the tallit is not part of everyday vestige, even today the Jewish people say that the tallit is a religious symbol, a garment, a shroud, a canopy, a cloak that envelopes the Jew both physically and spiritually in prayer and celebration, and in joy and in sorrow. The tallit is used at all major Jewish life events: circumcisions, *bar* and *bat mitzvahs,* weddings, and burials.

An interesting point to make at this juncture is that strictly observant Jewish men commonly wear a special four-cornered undergarment, called a *tallit katan* (little tallit), so to fulfill this important *mitzvah* (commandment) all day long. The tallit katan is worn under the shirt, with the tzitzit (tassels) hanging out so they can be seen.

The *tallit gadol* is the large tallit worn during prayers. It should be large enough to cover most of the wearer's body.

It is important to note that it is not the garment itself that makes the tallit special. The significance lies in the tzitzit, the fringes on the four corners. The purpose of the tallit, then, is to hold the tzitzit, and the purpose of the tzitzit, according to the Torah, is to remind us of God's commandments.

Jesus Healed on the Sabbath

Many years later, Jesus was accused of breaking the Sabbath commandment. In the following Scripture, we are privy to what happened that day:

> **One Sabbath day** *as Jesus was teaching in a synagogue, he saw a woman who had been crippled by an evil spirit. She had been bent double for eighteen years and was unable to stand up straight.* **When Jesus saw her, he called her over and said, "Dear woman, you are healed of your sickness!"** *Then he touched*

her, and instantly she could stand straight. How she praised God!

But the leader in charge of the synagogue was indignant that Jesus had healed her on the Sabbath day. *"There are six days of the week for working,"* he said to the crowd. *"Come on those days to be healed, not on the Sabbath."*

But the Lord replied, **"You hypocrites!** Each of you works on the Sabbath day! Don't you untie your ox or your donkey from its stall on the Sabbath and lead it out for water? **This dear woman, a daughter of Abraham, has been held in bondage by Satan for eighteen years. Isn't it right that she be released, even on the Sabbath?"**

This shamed his enemies, but all **the people rejoiced at the wonderful things he did** (Luke 13:10-17).

Jesus was not disobeying God's commandment, He was fulfilling it. Jesus said:

*"Don't misunderstand why I have come. I **did not come to abolish the law** of Moses or the writings of the prophets. No, **I came to accomplish their purpose"** (Matthew 5:17).

Jesus—our role model, the Man without sin, and the Son of God—brought a new covenant that doesn't disregard the past but builds on it for a better future for all, especially the hurting, disenfranchised, and forgotten people in the world.

Prayer

Lord God, the instructions You gave Your people in ancient days and in modern days are worthy of our serious consideration and adherence. Your declarations and actions are always with purpose. May we always seek to know Your intentions and to understand Your desires and will for us—that each will advance Your Kingdom. We know Your Word says in Isaiah 55:9 that Your ways are higher than ours and Your thoughts are also higher than ours, we plead for glimpses of Your ways and thoughts, Lord, so to know You and love You better. Blessed be the name of Jesus, Your Son, amen.

Chapter 3
What Are the Tzitzit?

As revealed in Chapter 2 and worth repeating, in ancient times, Hebrews were commanded to wear a tallit with tzitzits (tassels or fringes) as a continuous visual reminder to strengthen the holiness in their lives by remembering and practicing God's (YHVH's) commandments cited in Numbers 15:37-40 and Deuteronomy 22:12.

Tassels were to be tied onto the four corners of the tallit, or prayer shawl, to remind the Israelites of the commandments of YHVH. This was to ensure a symbol of the commandments was constantly before their eyes. Therefore, just looking at the tallit with its tzitzits, Jews were reminded of the commandments. It states in the Torah, *"When you see the tassels, you will remember and obey all the commands of the Lord, instead of following your own desires and defiling yourselves, as you are prone to do"* (Numbers 16:39).

Another translation for the word *tzitzit* is "wings," but we will discuss this in more detail in a later chapter.

Heavenly Blue

The blue color of the tzitzit was to remind the Jews of

the heavenly origin of the Law. It is interesting to note that God specifically mentions blue and how that color would serve as a reminder, *"...attach them with a blue cord"* (Numbers 15:38).

Throughout the Scriptures we can see, with study, that YHVH designed all of His creation to help reveal Himself to humankind. Jesus, God's Son *(Yeshua)*, taught spiritual truths using common physical things around Him to help His disciples understand Kingdom truths. Also, when the Scriptures were written, YHVH ensured that the stories held truths of the physical realm.

These stories, recounted in the Hebrew language, were all woven together to paint pictures that convey the spiritual truths that He designed for us to know. Usually these pictures are introduced at some point and then, through progressive revelation, we can see that they are built upon throughout the rest of the Holy Scriptures. These pictures can be unveiled with dedicated study—an essential part of being able to *"correctly explain the word of truth"* (2 Timothy 2:15).

Therefore, to understand the significance of the blue color used in the tzitzit, we need to remember that fringes are a YHVH-given reminder to His people. The shade of blue used on the fringes is called *tekhelet* in Hebrew.[1] Tekhelet is translated as the color of the heavens. Hence, the tekhelet serves as a reminder that

God's people are born from above and are called and required to reflect the nature of that heavenly Kingdom while we live here on earth.

The blue *tekhelet* thread originally had a purple hue of blue. The fluid was obtained from only one source, by extracting it from the gland of the murex trunculus snail. It took twelve thousand snails to fill a thimble-size container of blue dye.[2] The gland actually secretes a yellow fluid that, when exposed to sunlight, turns purple-blue and was used as a dye in biblical times.

Blue is the color of many items today, from paint to clothes to cake icing and tattoos. Because it is so readily available today, it is difficult to imagine that during the entire biblical period, blue was the most expensive color to produce. This is why it was reserved for only royalty. In 200 BC, one pound of blue-dyed cloth cost the equivalent of $36,000 today. By AD 300, this same pound of blue cloth would cost $96,000 today.[3] From these facts, we realize that Lydia, the seller of purple and an early convert to Christianity, was one of the wealthiest women in the empire.

> One of them was Lydia from Thyatira, a merchant of expensive purple cloth, who worshiped God. As she listened to us, the Lord opened her heart, and she accepted what Paul was saying (Acts 16:14).

After some time, the secret of this blue dye was lost; and so generally, the custom had been to use only white fringes. A group of researchers in Israel have claimed that they can identify this specific murex trunculus snail, and once again the blue dye is being manufactured.[4] However, not everybody accepts this as being the original tekhelet. More and more people put a blue thread among the fringes of their tallit, even though that practice is unacceptable in some Jewish communities because it isn't the true blue.

In 2014, a small cloth was discovered in Israel that is said to be 2,000 years old. It displays one of the very few remnants of the ancient tekhelet color. Over many years, researchers and rabbis have searched for more evidence of this rare dye with only two other discoveries. "It is believed that the fabrics discovered may have been part of the property belonging to Jewish refugees from the time of the Bar-Kokhba revolt against the Roman Empire of AD 132-135."[5] The Books of Chronicles mentions it as the veil in Solomon's Temple (see Exodus 26:31).

The Art of Tying

Tying the tzitzit is a Jewish art, which could be described as a specialized form of macramé. Macramé is the ancient art of tying knots.[6] It is an alternative form of textile making, using knotting rather than weaving or knitting. Its primary knots are the square knot and hitch knot. It has been used by sailors, especially in elaborate forms, to decorate the tools of their trade.

Four strands of thread are inserted through the reinforced hole in each corner of the tallit: three short strands and one long blue strand. The longer strand is called the *shamash* and is used for winding around the others. When done correctly, the tzitzit will have a pattern of first 7, then 8, then 11, and then 13 winds between the double knots. There are five double knots in total.[7]

It is important to note that the 7-8-11-13 winding pattern is significant. There are several interpretations for this pattern of winding. One interpretation is that each set of windings corresponds to one of the four letters in God's name.[8] Seven and eight equals fifteen, which in *gematria* (Jewish numerology) is equal to the two letters *yod* and *heh,* the first two letters of the name of God. Eleven is the equivalent of *vav* and *heh,* the last two letters of the name of God. Thus, they represent YHVH, the four-letter name of God. Thirteen is equivalent to the Hebrew word *echad (alef, chet, dalet),* which means one. Hence, all four windings can be interpreted to say, "God is One." So to look at the tzitzit is to remember and know that "God is One."

In gematria, the tzitzit (spelled *tzadi-yod-tzadi-yod-tav*) is equivalent to six hundred. To this we add the eight strands plus the five knots, totaling 613 in all. According to the Jewish tradition, God gave 613 *mitzvot* (commandments) in the Torah. Just to look at them, therefore, is to remember all the mitzvot.

The central commandment surrounding tzitzit is cited in Numbers 15:39 (NKJV): *"And you shall have the tassel, that you may **look upon it and remember** all the commandments of the Lord and do them...."*

Remember

We human beings seem to have very short memories. Our Father God knows this and He made provisions throughout His Word—Old and New Testaments—for us to remember Him, to help us focus on Him in the good and bad times. When we see something with our eyes, it jogs our memories and we remember this or that. The following are examples of how important it is to remember God's Word, and the stories in His Word. Each remembrance is to bring us closer to Him in some special way.

> *When I see the rainbow in the clouds, I will* **remember** *the eternal covenant between God and every living creature on earth* (Genesis 9:16).

Joseph pleaded with the cup-bearer, "And please **remember** me and do me a favor when things go well for you. Mention me to Pharaoh, so he might let me out of this place" (Genesis 40:14). But it was years later when the cup-bearer remembered and told Pharaoh about him. We would think that he would have been so thankful to Joseph for correctly interpreting his dream that he would have immediately told Pharaoh to have Joseph released, but no, we are a forgetful people.

"God also said to Moses, 'Say this to the people of Israel: Yahweh, the God of your ancestors—the God of Abraham, the God of Isaac, and the God of Jacob—has sent me to you. **This is my eternal name**, my name **to**

remember for all generations"' (Exodus 3:15). God many times uses others to help us remember. Here, God used Moses to tell the people that they are to remember His name for all generations. Did they? No, not everyone remembered. Do we? Not always.

God told the people in Exodus 20:23, **"Remember,** you must not make any idols of silver or gold to rival me." When we desire things above Him, we are making idols rise higher than God. He wants our full attention, not parts of it on Sunday morning or when we enter through church doors. When we focus on what gives us temporary pleasure or satisfaction, we are settling for less than the best—God gave us full-time pleasure, satisfaction, and eternal life.

"Treat them like native-born Israelites, and love them as you love yourself. **Remember** that you were once foreigners living in the land of Egypt. I am the Lord your God" (Leviticus 19:34). In our day, there are many foreigners worldwide traveling from many countries looking for refuge from persecution and economic distress. He tells us to love the foreigners, and I may add, using wisdom and discernment from above.

God has saved us from ourselves more times than we even can fathom and He has blessed us in more than a million ways. In Deuteronomy 7:19, we read: *"**Remember** the great terrors the Lord your God sent against them. You saw it all with your own eyes! And*

remember *the miraculous signs and wonders, and the strong hand and powerful arm with which he brought you out of Egypt. The Lord your God will use this same power against all the people you fear."* Our terrors may not be set as slaves in ancient Egypt but rather the rent or mortgage that is due and there is no money in the bank. Or a loved one is facing a terminal illness, or your spouse just left you. These are terrors that God will disperse by giving you comfort and peace as you face each terror together. And we must remember all the miraculous signs and wonders He places in front of us every day—the laughter of a child, the warm sunshine, the fresh air we breathe. Not a moment goes by that there isn't something to thank Him for.

God disperses terror.

The prophet Nehemiah tells us, "They refused to obey and **did not remember** the miracles you had done for them. Instead, they became stubborn and appointed a leader to take them back to their slavery in Egypt. **But you are a God of forgiveness, gracious and merciful, slow to become angry, and rich in unfailing love. You did not abandon them.**" Oh what a great God we serve! "They" means "us"—all of God's people have the choice of remembering and obeying or going our own way. We too often and too quickly choose the easy way out rather than God's way. We are stubborn and would rather be slaves in a world we know instead of being open to what God has in store for us—making us step out in faith, in Him.

David uses the word "remember" about fifty times in his psalms. David was a man after God's own heart so it stands to reason he would want to remember God and wanted God to remember him.

> *Do not **remember** the rebellious sins of my youth. **Remember** me in the light of your unfailing love, for you are merciful, O Lord (Psalm 25:7).*

> *My heart is breaking as I remember how it used to be: I walked among the house of God, singing for joy and giving thanks amid the sound of a great celebration! (Psalm 42:4).*

> ***Remember** that we are the people you chose long ago, the tribe you redeemed as your own special possession! And **remember** Jerusalem, your home here on earth (Psalm 74:2).*

> *But then I recall all you have done, O Lord; I **remember** your wonderful deeds of long ago (Psalm 77:11).*

> *For he knows how weak we are; he **remembers** we are only dust (Psalm 103:14).*

> *He causes us to **remember** his wonderful works. How gracious and merciful is our Lord! (Psalm 111:4)*

As in the Old Testament people were forgetful, we see nothing had changed from Psalms to the Gospels:

> The women were terrified and bowed with their faces to the ground. Then the men asked, "Why are you looking among the dead for someone who is alive? He isn't here! He is risen from the dead! **Remember** what he told you back in Galilee, that the Son of Man must be betrayed into the hands of sinful men and be crucified, and that he would rise again on the third day." Then they **remembered** that he had said this (Luke 24:5-8).

> *Then his disciples **remembered** this prophecy from the Scriptures; "Passion for God's house will consume me" (John 2:17).*

Jesus told us to remember as well:

> *Do you **remember** what I told you? "A slave is not greater than the master." Since they persecuted me, naturally they will persecute you. And if they had listened to me, they would listen to you (John 15:20).*

> *Yes, I'm telling you these things now, so that when they happen, you will **remember** my warning. I didn't tell you earlier because I was going to be with you for a while longer (John 16:4).*

Watch out! **Remember** *the three years I was with you—my constant watch and care over you night and day, and my many tears for you* (Acts 20:31).

And Paul cautions us to remember throughout his writings to believers—then and now:

Make allowance for each other's faults, and forgive anyone who offends you. **Remember,** *the Lord forgave you, so you must forgive others* (Colossians 3:13).

Always **remember** *that Jesus Christ, a descendant of King David, was raised from the dead. This is the Good News I preach* (2 Timothy 2:8).

As you endure this divine discipline, **remember** *that God is treating you as his own children. Who ever heard of a child who is never disciplined by its father?* (Hebrews 12:7)

James and others also tell us to remember...

And **remember,** *when you are being tempted, do not say, "God is tempting me." God is never tempted to do wrong, and he never tempts anyone else* (James 1:13).

And **remember** *that the heavenly Father to whom you pray has no favorites. He will judge or* *reward you according to what you do. So you must live in reverent fear of him during your time here as "temporary residents" (1 Peter 1:17).*

*Dear friend, don't let this bad example influence you. Follow only what is good. **Remember** that those who do good prove that they are God's children, and those who do evil prove that they do not know God (3 John 1:11).*

Prayer

Heavenly Father, as the early children of God were told to remember Your commands when they saw the color blue, may we remember Your commands when we see not only the color blue in the sky and the water but also the green of the grass and leaves and the black of the night and the sunlight of the morning. We thank You and remember You, Lord, for every color of the rainbow—the symbol of Your faithfulness and love.

Chapter 4
What Is the Atarah?

Tallitot usually have an artistic motif of some kind along the top neck portion. The motif or collar band is known as the *atarah* (crown). There is no particular religious significance to the atarah; it simply helps the wearer to hold the tallit the right way. However, it is common practice to write the words of a blessing on the tallit's atarah, so the person putting it on can read the blessing. Customarily, the person who uses the tallit says a blessing before he or she puts it on. The tallit is not blessed by rabbis—neither are any objects in the Jewish religion.

Note that some Jewish communities restrict the wearing of the tallit by women. And some are not in agreement with Christians wearing a tallit, yet we know that we are now grafted into the natural branches of God's family;

and in a respectful manner, Christians can reverently participate in Jewish traditions. Paul wrote to the church in Rome:

> Now **I am speaking to you Gentiles.** *Inasmuch then as I am an apostle to the Gentiles, I magnify my ministry in order somehow to make my fellow Jews jealous, and thus save some of them. For if their rejection means the reconciliation of the world, what will their acceptance mean but life from the dead? If the dough offered as firstfruits is holy, so is the whole lump, and* **if the root is holy, so are the branches.**
>
> **But if some of the branches were broken off, and you, although a wild olive shoot, were grafted in among the others and now share in the nourishing root of the olive tree, do not be arrogant toward the branches.** *If you are,* remember **it is not you who support the root, but the root that supports you.** *Then you will say, "Branches were broken off so that I might be grafted in." That is true. They were broken off because of their unbelief, but you stand fast through faith. So* **do not become proud, but fear. For if God did not spare the natural branches, neither will he spare you.**
>
> *Note then the kindness and the severity of God: severity toward those who have fallen, but*

God's kindness to you, provided you **continue in his kindness**. *Otherwise you too will be cut off. And even they, if they do not continue in their unbelief, will be grafted in, for* **God has the power to graft them in again.** *For* **if you were cut from what is by nature a wild olive tree, and grafted, contrary to nature, into a cultivated olive tree, how much more will these, the natural branches, be grafted back into their own olive tree** (Romans 11:13-24).

God's mercy is for everyone:

I want you to understand this mystery, dear brothers and sisters, so that you will not feel proud about yourselves. **Some of the people of Israel have hard hearts, but this will last only until the full number of Gentiles comes to Christ. And so all Israel will be saved.** As the Scriptures say, "The one who rescues will come from Jerusalem, and he will turn Israel away from ungodliness. And this is my covenant with them, that I will take away their sins" (Romans 11:25-27).

Paul, again writing to the believers in Rome, says:

For I am not ashamed of this Good News about Christ. It is the power of God at work, **saving everyone who believes—the Jew first and also**

the Gentile (Romans 1:16).

Blessings to God When Donning a Tallit

The following are examples of the blessings *(berachah)* that may be found embroidered on the atarah—the collar of the tallit. It needs to be stressed that these blessings are generally said aloud only when someone is placing a tallit around his or her shoulders.

Traditional Blessing

Blessed are You, Lord, our God, King of the universe, who has sanctified us with His commandments and commanded us to wrap ourselves in the tzitzit.

Transliteration: *Baruch atah Adonai, eloheinu, melekh ha'olam asher kiddeshanu bemitsvotav vetsivanu lehitattef batsitsit.*[1]

Messianic Blessing

Blessed are You, O Lord, King of the universe, who has fulfilled all of the law through Yeshua the Messiah and have covered us with His righteousness.

Transliteration: *Baruch atah Adonai, Eloheinu, melekh ha'olam asher milla et kol hatorah biyashu hamashiach iskissa et kulanu vetsedkator.*[2]

These blessings are prayers to the Lord, God, King of the universe. God hears every prayer from every person. In

Psalm 143:1, David knew that the Lord would listen to his plea, his prayer, and would answer *"because you* [God] *are faithful and righteous."* We can pray assured of God's undivided attention and His perfect answer in His perfect timing.

Blessings *from* God

Blessings *from* God are plentiful throughout the Bible. The word "blessing" means to declare happy and to speak well of. God blesses all people according to Matthew 5:45, *"In that way, you will be acting as true children of your Father in heaven. For he gives his sunlight to both the evil and the good, and he sends rain on the just and the unjust alike"*—but in particular, He blesses those who are in line with His commandments and will. For examples:

*"Taste and see that the Lord is good; **blessed** is the one who takes refuge in him"* (Psalm 34:8 NIV). Taking refuge in Him is to trust Him and lean on Him and not on our own understanding.

*"**Blessed** are those who have regard for the weak; the Lord delivers them in times of trouble"* (Psalm 41:1 NIV). Those who have are to share their resources—time, effort, resources—with those in need. This has been and should continue to be our agenda since the time of the Good Samaritan.

*"**Blessed** are those who listen to me, watching daily at my doors, waiting at my doorway"* (Proverbs 8:34 NIV). *"Now then, my children, listen to me; **blessed** are those who keep my ways"* (Proverbs 8:32 NIV). God wants to bless everyone who listens to Him and follows His plan for their lives. Keeping, obeying His commandments is the key to receive blessings from Him.

*"**Blessed** is the one who perseveres under trial because, having stood the test, that person will receive the crown of life that the Lord has promised to those who love him"* (James 1:12 NIV). Who would not want the *"crown of life"*? To receive such a prize, we must stand strong when faced with problems—we must have confidence in our God to bring us through every hard situation victorious!

"All praise to God, the Father of our Lord Jesus Christ, who has **blessed** us with every **spiritual blessing** in the heavenly realms because we are united with Christ" (Ephesians 1:3). Being united with Christ brings us special blessings—every spiritual blessing. Imagine that! Because believers are one with Jesus Christ, we have access to all spiritual blessings, which include peace of mind and heart, healing, Scripture awareness, discernment, and an intimate relationship with God.

And, of course, when the topic is blessedness, I must cite The Beatitudes, the words of Jesus when He delivered

His sermon on the Mount to the crowds and His disciples:

> **Blessed** *are the poor in spirit, for theirs is the kingdom of heaven.*
> **Blessed** *are those who mourn, for they will be comforted.*
> **Blessed** *are the meek, for they will inherit the earth.*
> **Blessed** *are those who hunger and thirst for righteousness, for they will be filled.*
> **Blessed** *are the merciful, for they will be shown mercy.*
> **Blessed** *are the pure in heart, for they will see God.*
> **Blessed** *are the peacemakers, for they will be called children of God.*
> **Blessed** *are those who are persecuted because of righteousness, for theirs is the kingdom of heaven.*
> **Blessed** *are you when people insult you, persecute you and falsely say all kinds of evil against you because of me. Rejoice and be glad, because* **great is your reward** *in heaven, for in the same way they persecuted the prophets who were before you* (Matthew 5:3-12 NIV).

There is no doubt that in some way all the people who were listening to Jesus that day were poor, mournful, meek, hungry and thirsty, merciful, pure in heart, peacemakers, persecuted, insulted, and badgered. Each of those with Him were in one way or another able to relate to what He was saying and knew Jesus was the Son of God. Who else could know their innermost feelings and thoughts. These blessings from Jesus touched their spirits and sparked hope in their hearts.

Prayers are your personal petitions to your heavenly Father.

Prayers are our personal petitions to our heavenly Father. When we make conscious efforts to obey, do what is right, and to trust God, we can know that He hears: *"The Lord is far from the wicked, but **he hears the prayers of the righteous"*** (Proverbs 15:29).

James tells us in the New Testament that we are to, **"Confess your sins** to each other and **pray for each other** so that you may be healed. The **earnest prayer of a righteous person has great power and produces wonderful results"** (James 5:16).

No matter if we are covering ourselves with a tallit or a suit coat or a t-shirt, let's pray "Thank You" to the good Lord who gave us His covering through the blood of Jesus. Then, let's thank Him for the clothes we have on our backs and in our closets. God is the Provider of all good things. He provides everything we need—not necessarily everything we want—to survive. Just as He provided the "total package" for Adam and Eve in the Garden of Eden, but they fell short of His expectations.

Even so, God provided clothing and shelter and food and water for the fallen couple. He continues to do so today for us. Therefore, as we slip into our shoes to go out, sit at the table for dinner or dash into the house from the rain, let's pray a thankful prayer for who He is and what He does for us each and every day.

Prayerful Connection

Prayer connects us with God and our spiritual selves. Prayer removes us from the physical hassles of the world and all its chaos. When seeking our heavenly Father through prayer, we are transported into a beautiful realm of peace and quiet. Taking time to contemplate is as beneficial today as it was when David wrote his Psalms and Paul contemplated the Lord's glory in 2 Corinthians 3:18 and John marveled at the revelations received from God.

Appreciate your blessings.

When we stop and consider all of our blessings, when we dig deeply into ourselves, it is not hard to realize that when we are obedient to His will and way in our lives, that is when we are the most at peace with ourselves and others.

There are times when we need to pray like Isaac, "*So today when I came to the spring, I prayed this prayer: 'O*

Lord, God of my master, Abraham, please give me success on this mission.'" We have many missions in life and asking God for success is reasonable. Whether at work or at home or at church, when we depend on the success God provides, we are assured of a perfect outcome.

And there are times when we need to take responsibility for our sins, as Ezra did, and pray to God honestly and openly, thanking Him for His grace and yet accepting His just and fair judgment:

> ... I fell on my knees with my hands spread out to the Lord my God and prayed:
>
> **"I am too ashamed and disgraced, my God, to lift up my face to you, because our sins are higher than our heads and our guilt has reached to the heavens.** From the days of our ancestors until now, our guilt has been great. Because of our sins, we and our kings and our priests have been subjected to the sword and captivity, to pillage and humiliation at the hand of foreign kings, as it is today.
>
> "But now, for a brief moment, **the Lord our God has been gracious** in leaving us a remnant and giving us a firm place in his sanctuary, and so our God gives light to our eyes and a little relief in our bondage. **Though we are slaves, our God has not forsaken us in our bondage.**

He has shown us kindness in the sight of the kings of Persia: **He has granted us new life** to rebuild the house of our God and repair its ruins, and **he has given us a wall of protection** in Judah and Jerusalem.

"But now, our God, what can we say after this? For **we have forsaken the commands** you gave through your servants the prophets when you said: 'The land you are entering to possess is a land polluted by the corruption of its peoples. By their detestable practices they have filled it with their impurity from one end to the other. Therefore, do not give your daughters in marriage to their sons or take their daughters for your sons. Do not seek a treaty of friendship with them at any time, that you may be strong and eat the good things of the land and leave it to your children as an everlasting inheritance.'

"**What has happened to us is a result of our evil deeds and our great guilt,** and yet, our God, **you have punished us less than our sins deserved** and have given us a remnant like this. Shall we then break your commands again and intermarry with the peoples who commit such detestable practices? Would you not be angry enough with us to destroy us, leaving us no remnant or survivor? **Lord, the God of Israel, you are righteous!** We are left this day as a remnant. Here we are before you in our guilt, though because of it **not one of us can stand in your presence**" (Ezra 9:5-15).

Ezra's prayer could be our prayer with only a few modifications. He was obviously aware of the people's sins and ashamed for them and himself. Knowing our wrongs and setting them right before God is the only way we know true freedom. He is more than willing to forgive us—we have to be more than willing to repent and ask for forgiveness.

Likewise, we must have forgiving hearts that will quickly forgive *any wrong* that *anyone* has ever done to us. If Jesus, our role model, can forgive His mockers, torturers, and executioners, we can surely forgive what has been done to us.

Jesus said, "Father, forgive them, for they don't know what they are doing" (Luke 23:34).

Prayer

Lord God, may we never cease to obey You and to respect Your people. May we forgive as You forgave. May Your commandments and traditions be our commandments and traditions, grafted into our heritage of faith. Moses received Your commandments for the good of the people—people then and people now—for benefit throughout the ages. May we seek forgiveness for our sins and always grant forgiveness to those who wrong us. We can only accomplish this attitude of forgiving with the help of the Holy Spirit. May He be ever near, ever willing to direct us. In the blameless name of Jesus who shed His blood for us, amen.

Chapter 5
Wearing a Tallit

A tallit is usually worn by a Jew who has reached the "age of majority" (commandment age), which is similar to "coming of age" or "age of maturity" in other cultures. In most Jewish communities, this would be the age of thirteen for a boy (*bar mitzvah—bar* meaning "son of" and *mitzvah* meaning "commandments)" and age twelve for a girl (*bat mitzvah—bat* meaning "daughter of" and *mitzvah* meaning "commandments"). These terms refer to both the individual reaching this age and to the ceremony that often accompanies this milestone.[1] This is the age when a young person is recognized as an adult.

It is interesting to note that traditionally the tallit was worn only by men, but with the development of non-orthodox movements (conservative and reform), more and more women are wearing a tallit for prayer.

When to Wear

It is a traditional practice that the tallit is worn only during the morning prayers, with the exception of the *Kol Nidre* service during Yom Kippur.[2]

Yom Kippur is the Sabbath of Sabbaths and is observed

on the tenth day of the Hebrew month of *Tishri*, which corresponds to September or early October in the secular calendar. It is the Jewish holiday of the Day of Atonement referenced in Exodus 30:10, Leviticus 16:29-30, Leviticus 23:27-31, Leviticus 25:9, and Numbers 29:7-11.

> Then the Lord said to Moses, "Be careful to celebrate the **Day of Atonement** on the tenth day of that same month—nine days after the Festival of Trumpets. You must observe it as an official day for holy assembly, a day to deny yourselves and present special gifts to the Lord. Do no work during that entire day because it is the **Day of Atonement,** when offerings of purification are made for you, making you right with the Lord your God (Leviticus 23:26-28).

The day is commemorated with a twenty-five-hour fast—specified as twenty-five hours and not twenty-four to ensure that the fast commences before the Sabbath begins. Individuals are supposed to refrain from eating and drinking even water and participate in intensive prayer. It is considered the holiest day of the Jewish year.

It is also important to note that Yom Kippur is a complete Sabbath, so all work is forbidden on this day. The fast begins before sunset on the evening before Yom Kippur and ends after nightfall on the day of Yom Kippur. It is a day to set aside to afflict the soul, to atone for the sins of the past year: *"It shall be to you a sabbath of solemn rest, and you shall afflict your souls; on the ninth day of the month at evening, from evening to evening, you shall celebrate your sabbath"* (Leviticus 23:32).

Ask for forgiveness for broken promises.

Simply put, Yom Kippur is the day to ask forgiveness for promises broken to God. The day before is reserved for asking forgiveness for broken promises between people.

In addition to the restrictions already mentioned, the following are also refrained from during Yom Kippur: anointing with perfumes or lotions, marital relations, wearing leather shoes, and bathing. Note that if a blessing is written on your tallit, you should not take the tallit into the bathroom with you. Sacred writings should not be taken into the bathroom. In Jewish communities, many synagogues have a tallit rack outside the bathroom. There will usually be a sign that tells you to remove your tallit before entering.

The evening service that begins Yom Kippur is commonly known as *Kol Nidre*, meaning "all vows." It is during this first service that the tallit is worn.

According to Jewish tradition, the act of putting on the tallit only has "religious merit" if it is done during daylight. Therefore, it is not normally worn at a Friday evening service, or any other evening service. It became customary to put on a tallit for Kol Nidre since it was still daylight at the time the service commenced. The tallit was then left on throughout the entire evening of the Yom Kippur service.

Therefore, although it is traditional that the tallit is only worn for morning prayers (during daylight), the exception of Kol Nidre is accepted along with two other occasions, one of which is the evening service of *Simchat Torah* (Rejoicing in the Torah). This holiday marks the completion of the annual cycle of weekly Torah readings with special Friday evening services that include a Torah reading as the Torah scrolls are then removed from the ark of the covenant.[3]

Right Heart Motives

In biblical times the Jewish men wore the prayer shawl all the time, not just at prayer. In New Testament times, ordinary people only wore a tallit on special occasions, if at all. It was the Pharisees who seem to have worn it regularly and, apparently in some cases, often for show. Jesus does not express disapproval of the custom itself, but He does condemn the extra-long fringes that the Pharisees wore to display their piety, declaring them hypocrites and therefore bad examples. Jesus told the people:

> When you pray, **don't be like the hypocrites who love to pray publicly** on street corners and

in the synagogues where everyone can see them. I tell you the truth, that is all the reward they will ever get. But when you pray, go away by yourself, shut the door behind you, and pray to your Father in private. Then your Father, who sees everything, will reward you (Matthew 6:5-6).

*Then Jesus said to the crowds and to his disciples, "The teachers of religious law and the Pharisees are the official interpreters of the law of Moses. So practice and obey whatever they tell you, **but don't follow their example.** For they don't practice what they teach. They crush people with unbearable religious demands and never lift a finger to ease the burden. Everything they do is for show. On their arms they wear extra wide prayer boxes with Scripture verses inside, and **they wear robes with extra long tassels**"* (Matthew 23:1-5).

*But all their works they do to be seen by men. They make their phylacteries broad and **enlarge the borders of their garments*** (Matthew 23:5 NKJV).

The word "phylacteries," or *tefillin*, does not appear in the Old Testament. Phylacteries appears only once in the New Testament. The word "phylacteries" is translated from the Greek word *phulakterion*, meaning a guard case or a leather pouch,[4] used in the instances cited in Matthew 23:5 for wearing scrolls of Torah passages.

Isolate yourself and focus on God.

Taking into consideration these Scriptures, we should ensure that the tallit is worn with the right motives of the heart to obtain the full spiritual benefit of this sacred tradition.

Wearing a tallit is still relevant today when you consider what we have learned so far. When you wrap yourself in the prayer shawl during prayer, you create your own personal space around yourself. The reason why it is good to create this private space is to isolate yourself from the environment and to keep you focused on God. By doing this you symbolically strengthen your commitment to your time of prayer with your Father in Heaven.

Donning the Tallit

Putting on the tallit is quite straightforward. Open or unfold your tallit and hold it in both hands so you can see the atarah. If the prayer shawl has the traditional blessings written on the atarah, it is customary to kiss the ends of the neckband where the last word and the first word of the blessing are written. Recite the blessing.

After reciting the blessing, swing the tallit over your head and bring your hands together in front of your face, briefly covering your head with the tallit for a moment of private meditation. Then adjust the tallit comfortably on your shoulders like a cape.

If you are thinking of wearing a tallit during your prayer time or in reverence to God, there are several Scriptures on which you can meditate. The following verses in Psalm 104 are very popular and spoken often:

Let all that I am praise the Lord. O Lord my God, how great you are! You are robed with honor and majesty. You are dressed in a robe of light. You stretch out the starry curtain of the heavens; you lay out the rafters of your home in the rain clouds. You make the clouds your chariot; you ride upon the wings of the wind. O Lord, what a variety of things you have made! In wisdom you have made them all. The earth is full of your creatures. May the glory of the Lord continue forever! The Lord takes pleasure in all he has made! The earth trembles at his glance; the mountains smoke at his touch. I will sing to the Lord as long as I live. I will praise my God to my last breath! May all my thoughts be pleasing to him, for I rejoice in the Lord. Let all sinners vanish from the face of the earth; let the wicked disappear forever. Let all that I am praise the Lord. Praise the Lord! (Psalm 104:1-3,24,31-35)

Reciting prayers and blessings should not become rote—without meaning, drudgery. Reciting prayers and blessings are privileges that we must consider sacred. Saying them aloud makes them even more special as we hear ourselves talking to our Lord God, knowing that He is listening.

Even through Persecution

Most people worldwide can pray aloud without fear, yet many Christians in certain countries are persecuted for acknowledging their faith in God.

An article in *The Washington Times* dated February 7, 2017, states:

> From the Coptics in Egypt and the 'house churches' in China to the 'subversives' in North Korea and the 'apostates' in Pakistan, Christians are under fire on the international stage. Paul Coleman, deputy director of the Alliance Defending Freedom International, said the international persecution of Christians is unrivalled. 'No person or group should live in fear of being killed, tortured or oppressed because of their religious beliefs,' Mr. Coleman said in a statement. 'By all accounts Christians are the most persecuted group on the planet.'
>
> Each month, about 322 Christians are killed, 214

churches or Christian properties are destroyed, and 772 acts of violence are carried out on Christians because of their faith, according to Open Doors, a non-profit group that helps persecuted Christians.[5]

Anti-Semitism is just as rampant. In the United Kingdom, "anti-Semitism in the UK reached 'unprecedented' levels in 2016, after a rise of 36 percent in the number of incidents. …with 1,309 incidents reported last year—the highest on record."[6] The Anti-Defamation League, which tracks religious persecution, cites only a few of the countries where numerous violent and deadly anti-Semitic incidents occurred in 2014: Argentina, Australia, Belgium, Brazil, Bulgaria, Canada, Denmark, France, Germany, Greece, Hungary, Ireland, Italy, Mexico, Morocco, The Netherlands, Norway, Russia, South Africa, Sweden, Spain, Switzerland, Tunisia, Turkey, Ukraine, United Kingdom, Uruguay, Venezuela, and New Zealand.[7]

Our Christian faith is founded in the Jewish faith—our Savior is a Jew, His family was Jewish. As we move on in our study of the tallit and biblical truths, may we remember that God shows no favoritism; He created each person as a unique individual, He loves each of us and wants all to know Him as Lord and Savior, desiring none to perish. We should have the same mindset as God.

Then Peter replied, "I see very clearly that God shows no favoritism" (Acts 10:34).

For God does not show favoritism (Romans 2:11).

And the leaders of the church had nothing to add to what I was preaching. (By the way, their reputation as great leaders made no difference to me, for God has no favorites.) (Galatians 2:6).

Masters, treat your slaves in the same way. Don't threaten them; remember, you both have the same Master in heaven, and he has no favorites (Ephesians 6:9).

But if you do what is wrong, you will be paid back for the wrong you have done. For God has no favorites (Colossians 3:25).

I solemnly command you in the presence of God and Christ Jesus and the highest angels to obey these instructions without taking sides or showing favoritism to anyone (1 Timothy 5:21).

My dear brothers and sisters, how can you claim to have faith in our glorious Lord Jesus Christ if you favor some people over others? (James 2:1)

In the same way, it is not my heavenly Father's will that even one of these little ones should perish (Matthew 18:14).

For this is how God loved the world: He gave his one and only Son, so that everyone who believes in him will not perish but have eternal life
(John 3:16).

Whether acknowledging our faith aloud in church, at the dinner table, or silently in our prayer closets, our communication with God the Father is a sacred time when we exchange our worldly trappings for His spiritual covering. And whether we put on a tallit or not, we should feel free to enter the Lord's gates with the thanksgiving and praise that He deserves and expects of His children.

Prayer

Lord God, we appreciate and respect and try to obey the commandments You gave to Moses for the people of Israel. We ask that You give us the wisdom to know how to please You and what You expect of us. May we ever be seeking Your face and Your will for our lives. As we look to You for the meaning of our lives, we trust You implicitly to show us the way—Your way. Father, we humbly pray that You will protect those who oppose and persecute You in Heaven and your family here on earth. Remove the evil from hearts bent on harming the innocents worldwide. We ask all this in the holy name of Jesus, amen.

Chapter 6
The Tallit: The Covering

In Middle Eastern culture, it was tradition for the man to cast a garment over the woman being claimed for marriage. This was clearly demonstrated in the Bible when Ruth lay at the feet of Boaz.

> Around midnight Boaz suddenly woke up and turned over. He was surprised to find a woman lying at his feet! "Who are you?" he asked. "I am your servant Ruth," she replied. **"Spread the corner of your covering over me**, for you are my family redeemer" (Ruth 3:8-9).

The tallit is often used as a covering over the bride and bridegroom during a Jewish wedding ceremony (traditionally called Kiddushin).[1] The tallit forms a canopy under which the couple stands. The wedding ceremony is performed under the tallit, which is held up by four poles called chuppah or huppah.

One custom is to have honored friends hold the chuppah poles. In some families, the custom is to make a family chuppah and to pass it down from generation to generation (as opposed to a wedding dress). The chuppah represents the home that they will create together and the Divine Presence under which they will be married.

During the final benediction, the couple is wrapped in two tallitots that are placed around their shoulders. In some Jewish communities, the bride and groom are wrapped together by a single tallit. In others, the bridegroom covers his bride with his tallit, signifying that he is taking her into his care.

Allow the Divine Presence to reign over your home.

The groom will continue to use the tallit during his married life and would hope to present it to a future son upon his bar mitzvah. Also, often the children born to the couple will be wrapped in the same tallit when they are named.

There is also a custom that the bride presents the groom with a tallit on the day of the wedding. This is because the tallit also represents the number thirty-two, which is the number of fringes on the shawl. The number thirty-two is the numerical equivalent of the Hebrew word for heart. [2]

Head Coverings

In keeping with our study of Jewish traditions and our intention to gain knowledge, an interesting topic is head coverings for men and women of the faith. Rabbi Adin Steinsaltz's guide to Jewish headcoverings, a portion follows, is directed at the newly observant Jew in an Orthodox setting who must decide what head covering he or she is going to wear, and under what circumstances:[3]

> Talmudic law does not require covering the head, though there are hints that doing so is to be regarded as a sign of reverence. But the practice became more and more widespread, until by the Middle Ages Jewish legal authorities everywhere were unanimous that sacred words (prayers, words of Torah) could not be spoken, nor sacred precincts (synagogues, houses of study, even cemeteries) entered bareheaded. Today, too, there is complete *halakhic* [Jewish legal] agreement on this question.
>
> Covering the head at all times is a different matter. In Europe, it was the universal custom among Orthodox Jews, except for some in Germany, to do so indoors and out. The most orthodox even did it while sleeping. In the Near East there was greater latitude in the matter, and many religious Jews only covered their heads for sacred activities. Keeping the head covered at all times has a *kabbalistic* [mystical] significance, leading some to cover their heads twice—a hat over a *kippah*

(skullcap), or a *tallit (prayer shawl)* over a *kippah*—while praying.

Male Head Covering: Religious Meaning from Social Consensus

It is for this reason that covering the head has become significant and valuable, not because it has any inherent meaning but rather as a conventional sign of belonging to a certain group of people and of commitment to a certain way of life. The [newly observant Jew] must be aware of this symbolism. On the one hand, if he does not cover his head, he will be regarded by the Orthodox (particularly in Israel) as a deviant from the true path, no matter how observant he is. On the other hand, if he is not fully observant, at least in public, the fact that he covers his head may lead others to see him as hypocritical. Indeed, it may cast a shadow of hypocrisy over the entire observant community. Thus, [for a man] covering the head is an act fraught with significance that must be weighed very seriously.

Women's Head Coverings: A Sign of Marital Status

In the case of women, too, there is, in addition to a general requirement of modesty of dress, a specific one concerning covering the head. Married women are required to cover their hair. This is an ancient law, already hinted at in the Torah, that has been observed among Jews all through the ages. In some communities, even unmarried women have been known to keep their hair covered, though this custom never became widespread. The law is not related to that requiring men to cover their heads, and it is even more stringent. The fact that a married woman covers her hair whenever she leaves the house is a sign of her special status.

In recent times it has become customary for women to cover their hair with wigs, and this can indeed be seen as fulfilling the requirements of the *halakhah*. Married women are not, after all, expected to make themselves "ugly." Nevertheless, there have been scholars who have ruled that wigs too must be covered, particularly when they look so natural that they cannot be recognized as head coverings and the women who wear them are not recognizable as married. But this too is a matter of custom and not of definitive *halakhah*.

Covering the Head as a Spiritual Statement

In Jewish tradition, and even in very old linguistic usage, "an uncovered head" means unbridled license. By the same token, covering the head, be it for prayer and study or at any other time, represents, by general usage at least, the acceptance of Divine sovereignty, of the "yoke of the kingdom of heaven."

I find this excerpt from the rabbi especially interesting in view of the strong statements the apostle Paul makes in the New Testament when he wrote to the believers in Corinth:

A man dishonors his head if he covers his head while praying or prophesying. But a woman dishonors her head if she prays or prophesies without a covering on her head, for this is the same as shaving her head. Yes, if she refuses to wear a head covering, she should cut off all her hair! But since it is shameful for a woman to have her hair cut or her head shaved, she should wear a covering.

A man should not wear anything on his head when worshiping, for man is made in God's image and reflects God's glory. *And woman reflects man's glory. For the first man didn't come from woman, but the first woman came from man. And man was not made for woman,* *but woman was made for man. For this reason, and because the angels are watching, **a woman should wear a covering on her head to show she is under authority.***

But among the Lord's people, women are not independent of men, and men are not independent of women. For although the first woman came from man, every other man was born from a woman, and everything comes from God.

***Judge for yourselves.** Is it right for a woman to pray to God in public without covering her head? Isn't it obvious that it's disgraceful for a man to have long hair? And isn't long hair a woman's pride and joy? For it has been given to her as a covering. But if anyone wants to argue about this, I simply say that we have no other custom than this, and neither do God's other churches* (1 Corinthians 11:2-16).

As Paul says, we are to judge for ourselves, which is what the modern-day church has done. Gone are the days of church-goers wearing their "Sunday best" clothes. Now the norm is for people to "be comfortable." Come-as-you-are attitudes permeate churches worldwide. I believe the attitude of the heart of the people is what truly matters. If someone attends church in formal attire and someone else walks in who just came from working all night and they both sincerely worship God and praise Him, I doubt the Father is going to be anything but pleased to see those two in His House—head covering or not.

Prayer Covering

When we pray for someone, we are covering them with the blessings of God, the promises of God. For example, if someone asks for prayer because he or she is ill, when we immediately pray with that person, our prayers not only reach the Great Physician, but also touch the heart of the person we are praying with. Most people feel a sense of peace and serenity when they know they are being covered in prayer.

Prayers for others is called intercessory prayer and as we offer up our prayers, Jesus intercedes for us before the Father, Jesus *"is sitting in the place of honor at God's right hand, pleading for us"* (Romans 8:34). So not only are our prayers being heard by God, Jesus is adding His favor to them as well!

Pray for others as well as yourself.

In the Old Testament, a Levitical priest was the intermediary between the people and God. He would be the one to offer sacrifices on behalf of the people to the Lord—standing between a righteous God and sinful humankind. Then in the Word of God's New Testament it says:

> So if the priesthood of Levi, on which the law was based, could have achieved the perfection God intended, why did God need to establish a different priesthood, with a priest in the order of Melchizedek instead of the order of Levi and Aaron?
>
> And if the priesthood is changed, the law must also be changed to permit it. For the priest we are talking about belongs to a different tribe, whose members have never served at the altar as priests. What I mean is, our Lord came from the tribe of Judah, and Moses never mentioned priests coming from that tribe.
>
> This change has been made very clear since a different priest, who is like Melchizedek, has appeared. **Jesus became a priest, not by meeting the physical requirement of belonging to the tribe of Levi, but by the power of a life that cannot be destroyed.** And the psalmist pointed this out when he prophesied, "You are a priest forever in the order of Melchizedek."
>
> Yes, **the old requirement about the priesthood was set aside** because it was weak and useless. For the law never made anything perfect. **But now we**

> **have confidence in a better hope, through which we draw near to God** (Hebrews 7:11-19).

This Scripture passage tells us that believers, through our spiritual birth as new creatures in Christ, are the new order of priests with Jesus as the High Priest. Now Jesus stands between the people and God—He is our intermediary. We can approach Him through the shed blood of the High Priest, Jesus. No longer does the Priest have to sacrifice the blood of animals—Jesus sacrificed His blood for our salvation.

Holiness and righteousness is the necessary requirement to stand before the Lord. Are we holy and righteous? No, not as the fallen creatures we are. But yes, as the redeemed of the Lord!

The Bible tells us, **"Confess your sins** *to each other and* **pray for each other** *so that you may* **be healed.** *The earnest prayer of a righteous person has great power and produces wonderful results"* (James 5:16).

This verse in James 5 is very clear about what we are expected to do to be healed and what sincere prayers by righteous people will produce. Whether healing comes to the body, spirit, mind, relationships, or whatever is in need of curing, when we confess our sins (we all have them) and pray for each other, healing will be the result.

"Wonderful results" include miracles, God-given good health, being set free from sin and troubles, and a host of other enjoyable outcomes! To set our minds on this verse means our entire perspective of life will change—for the better. The Bible is full of verse after verse of wisdom. When we seriously study the Word of God, there is no better result than to be full of the knowledge of His ways and His will. Our Creator God's magnificence can only be realized when we take the time to explore Him through His Word.

When we seek God in His Word and pray for His covering at the same time, there is no limit to how intimately He will meet us. When the Lord Jesus' words are rattling around and around in our minds and praises are constantly stirring within our spirits, then we will feel the spiritual tallit wrapped around us—covering us with His love and mercy.

> In all their suffering he [God] also suffered, and he personally rescued them. In his **love and mercy** he redeemed them. He lifted them up and carried them through all the years (Isaiah 63:9).

Agonizing Prayer

When Jesus prayed before going to make the ultimate sacrifice, He "prayed more fervently, and he was in such agony of spirit that his sweat fell to the ground like great drops of blood" (Luke 22:44).

Jesus was praying that His heavenly Father would "take this cup of suffering away from me. Yet I want your will to be done, not mine" (Luke 22:42). As finite human beings, we cannot fathom the depth of Jesus' prayer and His response to the horrible death He was facing. Our simple minds cannot begin to understand the magnitude of His agony, yet total compliance with God's plan for Him and for all humankind. But God knew—and He sent an angel from Heaven to strengthen Jesus.

Pray so you will not give in to temptation.

Even with impending torture and painful death just ahead, Jesus told His disciples twice to pray: *"Pray that you will not give in to temptation"* (Luke 22:40) and *"Get up and pray, so that you will not give in to temptation"* (Luke 22:46). Why was Jesus so intent on making sure that His disciples pray against being tempted? Perhaps because He knew they were—and we are—so very easily tempted by the evil of the world.

Jesus cares so much about His followers that He pushed away His agony to instruct them. What did they do? Rather than praying, they fell asleep. How often do we receive guidance from the Holy Spirit and rather than following through, we get distracted—or fall asleep. Jesus knew then and knows now that we human beings are fallible and fickle. There is no trying to fake our motives, attitudes, or intentions. We must be honest, with ourselves and with God.

Apostle Paul knew this when he wrote to the believers in Rome:

> *I don't really understand myself, for I want to do what is right, but I don't do it.* Instead, I do what I hate. *But if I know that what I am doing is wrong, this shows that I agree that the law is good. So I am not the one doing wrong; it is sin living in me that does it.* And I know that *nothing good lives in me,* that is, in my sinful nature. I want to do what is right, but I can't. I want to do what is good, but I don't. I don't want to do what is wrong, but I do it anyway. *But if I do what I don't want to do, I am not really the one doing wrong; it is sin living in me that does it.*
>
> I have discovered this *principle of life*—that when I want to do what is right, I inevitably do what is wrong. I love God's law with all my heart. But *there is another power within me that is at war with my mind.* This power makes me a slave to the sin that is still within me. Oh, what a miserable person I am! *Who will free me from this life that is*

***dominated by sin and death? Thank God!
The answer is in Jesus Christ our Lord.*** *So
you see how it is: In my mind I really want to
obey God's law, but because of my sinful
nature I am a slave to sin* (Romans 7:15-25).

Unlike you and me, Jesus was no slave to sin. He came
to this world to free us from sin, yet we will struggle
with this *"principle of life"* until He comes to take us
home, or we go to our heavenly home before He
comes. Daily we must *"Fight the good fight for the true
faith. Hold tightly to the eternal life to which God has
called you"* (1 Timothy 6:12).

When faced with a terminal illness or a serious sickness
of a loved one, we, like Jesus can turn to God in prayer,
knowing that He hears us and will answer us. He will
cover us with His mercy, and we, in turn, must have faith
and trust that His good and perfect purpose will prevail.

Prayer

Lord God Almighty, please send angels to cover
and strengthen us, as You did for Jesus, when we
are too tired to pray, or too distracted, or too
worried about what tomorrow will bring. May we
take the advice of Jesus to pray so we are not
tempted—tempted by the evil one whose goal it
is to destroy us—to devour us whole, or little by
little, sin by sin. "Stay alert! Watch out for your

great enemy, the devil. He prowls around like a roaring lion, looking for someone to devour" (1 Peter 5:8). We know that You who is in us is greater than the evil of the world. We thank You and praise You for that assurance!

Chapter 7
The Tallit: The Mantle

As previously mentioned, the tallit is also known as a cloak, robe, coat, or mantle, and that it was a commandment of God that the four corners of the garment have tzitzits, or tassels, attached so that God's people would be constantly reminded to obey His Law. Realizing this, we can see various places in the Scriptures where the tallit is mentioned and the implications or relevance of the events that occur.

For example, in 1 Samuel 15, we read about Samuel the prophet informing Saul that he is no longer king of Israel.

> But Samuel replied, "I will not go back with you! Since you have rejected the Lord's command, he has rejected you as king of Israel." As Samuel turned to go, **Saul tried to hold him back and tore the hem of his robe.** And Samuel said to him, "The Lord has torn the kingdom of Israel from you today and has given it to someone else—one who is better than you" (1 Samuel 15:26-28).

It is clearly not a coincidence that in Saul's distress he grabbed hold of Samuel's mantle, or more specifically, the skirt of the mantle (representing God's Law), which is translated "wing," the *tzitzit*. He grabbed so tightly that Samuel's mantle tore. Samuel makes it clear that because Saul rejected the Word of the Lord, the commandment of God, he had been rejected as king. Furthermore, just as he tore the mantle, the kingship would be torn from him.

Scripture suggests that mantles are transferred or passed on to a successor, son, designated relative, or servant.

> Anyone who escapes from Hazael will be killed by Jehu, and those who escape Jehu will be killed by Elisha! Yet I will preserve 7,000 others in Israel who have never bowed down to Baal or kissed him!" So Elijah went and found Elisha son of Shaphat plowing a field. There were twelve teams of oxen in the field, and Elisha was plowing with the twelfth team. **Elijah went over to him and threw his cloak across his shoulders and then walked away** (1 Kings 19:17-19).

In 1 Kings 19, God speaks to Elijah and makes it clear that his successor is to be Elisha, so Elijah goes and finds Elisha and casts his cloak, his mantle, on him. Elisha recognizes the call of God on his life and leaves everything to follow Elijah. When Elijah's ministry comes to an end, the anointing that comes to rest on Elisha is that of Elijah and of Elijah's mantle. Many believe that Elijah's mantle was symbolic of the *power of prayer* with which Elijah had saturated it.

> Then Elijah folded his cloak together and struck the water with it. The river divided, and the two of them went across on dry ground! ... Elisha picked up Elijah's cloak, which had fallen when he was taken up. Then Elisha returned to the bank of the Jordan River. He struck the water with Elijah's cloak and cried out, "Where is the Lord, the God of Elijah?" Then the river divided, and Elisha went across. When the group of prophets from Jericho saw from a distance what happened, they exclaimed, "Elijah's spirit rests upon Elisha!" And they went to meet him and bowed to the ground before him (2 Kings 2:8,13-15).

The words of Zechariah in the Scripture passage that follows are particularly profound, demonstrating that all nations will embrace and reverence the Word of the Lord, the commandment of God, which is depicted by taking a firm hold of the hem of his robe mentioned in Zechariah 8.

The majority of Jewish points of reference (such as rabbinical sources, sages throughout the ages, and Jewish writing and commentary), stress the fact that the commandments or Law were given to the Jews. Because of this, the tallit, and more significantly the tzitzit, are considered in many circles irrelevant to the Gentile (non-Jew).[1]

However, I believe that this passage in Zechariah 8 demonstrates to us that Christians worldwide, of all nations and tongues, will be drawn to the ancient language of God and therefore ancient truths that have been overlooked.

> This is what the Lord Almighty says: **"Many peoples and the inhabitants of many cities will yet come, and the inhabitants of one city will go to another and say, 'Let us go at once to entreat the Lord and seek the Lord Almighty.** I myself am going.' And **many peoples and powerful nations will come to Jerusalem to seek the Lord Almighty** and to entreat him."
> This is what the Lord Almighty says: "In those days ten **people from all languages and nations will take firm hold of one Jew by the hem of his robe and say, 'Let us go with you, because we have heard that God is with you'"** (Zechariah 8:21-23 NIV).

It is not by coincidence that today so many non-Jews have begun a journey of discovery that literally brings the Scriptures to life. No matter how many times you read the Bible or hear the Word being taught, the Holy Spirit will drop a new revelation into your heart and spirit for comfort, wisdom, peace, an answer, or whatever you need at that moment.

Torah Safekeeping

In the Jewish community, a type of mantle is also used to cover and store the Torah when it is not being read. The Torah is handwritten in Hebrew, the oldest Jewish language. It is also called the Law of Moses *(Torat Moshe)*. The Torah primarily refers to the first five books of the Hebrew Scriptures: Genesis, Exodus, Leviticus, Numbers, and Deuteronomy. The Torah is also known as the Five Books of Moses or the Pentateuch (Greek for "five containers," which refers to the scroll cases in which the books were being kept).

For Jews, the Torah is traditionally accepted as the literal word of God as told to Moses. A portion of it is read each week in the synagogue. It takes a year to complete the readings.[2]

The Torah mantle is typically made of luxurious fabrics with intricate embroidery symbolic of key events in Jewish history, demonstrating the unique style of Jewish art. The Torah mantle's sole use is to cover and protect the Torah it contains. Traditionally, the Torah is kept in a curtained-off area known as the ark of Law.

The rabbi lifts the Torah and its mantle out of this space in front of the congregation.

The Jewish Virtual Library provides more insight:

> The Torah mantle is as it were the clothing of the Torah scroll. In Sephardi communities, Italy, and Germany, and in halakhic literature, it was indeed occasionally known as beged, "garment," or mappah, but later the term me'il became standard in most communities. The earliest attestation to the shape of the mantle appears in the 14th-century Sarajevo Haggadah, created in Spain. The mantles shown there are made of a costly material, probably not embroidered. This tradition is still common today in Sephardi communities, with the exception of Morocco and Algeria, where Torah mantles are made of velvet with elaborately embroidered patterns and dedicatory inscriptions. Common motifs on these mantles are the Tree of Life (in Morocco) and a gate (in Algeria). The shapes of the mantle differ from community to community—some are wide and open in the front (Italy and the Spanish Diaspora), others have a small cape atop the robe, still others are of simple rectangular length with material gathered at the upper borders (Algeria).

The earliest German mantles are depicted in

15th-century manuscripts. This Torah mantle is generally narrower and smaller than the Sephardi mantle, while the robe-like part is made of two rectangular lengths of material sewn together. Two openings at the upper end of the mantle enable the staves to protrude. The designs on Torah mantles in Germany and Central Europe are influenced by the ornamentation of the Torah Ark curtain, with such motifs as a pair of columns, lions, and the Torah crown most frequent.[3]

Creation began with God's command, *"Let there be light,"* signifying the beginning of the divine light of God in the world (Genesis 1:3). It seems logical that the Torah is often described in imagery as light. For example, *Torah Orah* means "the Teaching of Light."[4]

Why mention the Torah mantle at all? It becomes clear from study that it is completely different from the tallit. The relevance is simple. The main purpose of the tallit is to hold the tzitzit. The main purpose of the tzitzit is to remind us of the commandments of Yahweh. It seems apt, therefore, to ensure that we understand what the commandments of Yahweh are or at least know where we can find them, as the Torah contains the Law of God.

Reminders

Anything that reminds us of God's commandments is a

good thing. Referring back to the beginning of the book and how a man was stoned to death for "working" on the Sabbath by picking up sticks, although we are not subject to physical death as was the man, the more we remember His commandments and keep them, the more alive spiritually we will be.

Perhaps hanging a tassel in your home or car or at work—or all three places—is a good idea. Each will be a reminder of God's love and mercy—and that He wants you to obey the Ten Commandments, given to you for the benefit of your health and welfare. Although it would not be authentic, you could make a tzitzit, a tassel, yourself or buy one at a local store or online as a symbol of your desire to remember His commands.

In the United States, there has been decades-long litigation, court battles, and public outcry regarding the public display of the Ten Commandments. In one of the first and most controversial incidents, Chief Justice Roy Moore of the state of Alabama in the US was adamant that a Ten Commandments monument in the rotunda of an Alabama state judicial building remain as a reminder of "our very source of our rights and liberties and the very source of our law."[5] Although he faced vicious opposition, Judge Moore was eventually suspended for holding his ground; and on August 27, 2003, the monument was forcibly removed. "God has chosen this time and this place so we can save our country and save our courts for our children," Moore said.[6] Moore and his supporters stated that forbidding the acknowledgment of the Judeo-Christian God violates the First Amendment's guarantee of free exercise of religion. The day after the ruling, a poll taken by two respected media outlets indicated that 77 percent of Americans "disapproved of the US District Judge Myron Thompson's order to remove the monument."[7]

More recently, in 2015, one of the many battles for keeping the Ten Commandments in public view involved the governor of the state of Oklahoma who defied a court order to remove the Ten Commandments monument from the Capitol grounds.

> In May, Aaron Cooper, spokesman for Oklahoma's Attorney General, argued that the Ten Commandments monument was not serving a religious purpose. "The Ten Commandments has played a historical role in the founding of this nation," said Mr. Cooper, "And because it honors the historical role of the commandments, the Ten Commandments monument on the Oklahoma Capitol grounds is constitutional." As far as the "historic purpose" justification goes, "the Ten Commandments are obviously religious in

nature and are an integral part of the
Jewish and Christian faiths," justices
stated in Tuesday's ruling.[8]

Why all the controversy? The evil one knows that if
people don't see the Ten Commandments, they will
forget them, forget the Lord. People remember what
they see—as in the command to attach tzitzits to the
tallit, as reminders.

Franklin Graham, son of well-known evangelist Bill
Graham, was outraged at the Oklahoma ruling to
remove the Ten Commandments. A portion of an
article reveals his angst:

America is not only "blatantly defying
God's laws," it's trying to erase them from
public view, evangelist preacher Franklin
Graham charges in a blistering
condemnation of an Oklahoma court order
to remove a Ten Commandments
monument.

The president of the foundation named
after his famed father Billy Graham and
leader of the global charity Samaritan's
Purse, writes in a Facebook post that
"everything related to God and His Word"
is lately coming under fire.

"When I went to school, the Ten Commandments were posted in the classroom, and the teacher led us in the Lord's Prayer before we went to lunch," he writes. "There was respect throughout society for the Word of God. How times have changed!"

"These days," he continues, "everything related to God and His Word is coming under fire in our nation. We're living in a time when our country is not only blatantly defying God's laws, but is trying to remove them completely from public view. Just think what a difference it would make if our school children today learned about the Ten Commandments and and the God who wrote them."

In particular, Graham rails at the Oklahoma Supreme Court ruling on Tuesday that ordered the removal of a 6-foot-tall Ten Commandments monument on the capitol grounds.[9]

From New Mexico to Alabama to Idaho, over the past several decades, people across the United States have expressed their anger at the removal of principles that provide the foundation and stability of a civil society. Yet it seems the masses are held captive by a few.

No doubt this controversy will continue as more and more public displays of God Almighty are removed. Yet our love and devotion to God the Father cannot be removed from our hearts. It is no surprise that God provided a way for us to remember His commandments and covenants within ourselves when the world strives to distract us.

We can cover ourselves in our mantles and concentrate on Him whether or not His commandments are posted here or there. It takes more effort on our part to seek and find and intentionally focus on Him nowadays, but we must *remember.*

Take Up Their Mantles

As Elisha took up the mantle of Elijah, we must take up the mantle of faithful Christians before us. For example, several Christians in particular come to mind: Abraham Lincoln, William Wilberforce, Corrie Ten Boom and her family, Dietrich Bonhoeffer, Abraham Lincoln, Martin Luther King Jr., William and Catherine Booth, and Nelson Mandela who risked their lives to tangibly show God's mercy and love for freedom and equal rights for all people.

Dietrich Bonhoeffer was a German Protestant theologian who was caught up in the era of Nazism and the egregious use of Christianity as a prop for Adolf Hitler's fury against the Jewish people. Described as "pastor, martyr, prophet, and spy" by author Eric

Metaxas in his best-selling book on Bonhoeffer, he was this and more. Bonhoeffer was one of the first to speak out against Hitler and saw first-hand how the cruel dictator used the church for his own evil endeavors.

Bonhoeffer was the leading spokesman for the Confessing Church, which was the center of the German Protestant resistance to the Nazi regime. At one point, Bonhoeffer "proposed to create a clear statement of faith to force the German Christians to define themselves" according to times. He went to Bethel, a community in Biesenthal, Germany, to work on writing the confession. His time there is worth mentioning:

> As much as he [Bonhoeffer] had heard about this fabled place, he was quite unprepared for what he saw. Bethel (Hebrew for "house of God") had begun in 1867 as a Christian community for people with epilepsy, but by 1900 included several facilities that cared for sixteen hundred disabled persons. Bonhoeffer had never seen anything like it. It was the gospel made visible, a fairy-tale landscape of grace, where the weak and helpless were cared for in a palpably Christian atmosphere. Yet even in 1933, the anti-gospel of Hitler was moving toward the legal murder of these people who, like the Jews, were categorized as unfit, as a

drain on Germany. The terms increasingly used to describe these people with disabilities were *useless eaters* and *life unworthy of life.*[10]

A scholar and man of wealth, Bonhoeffer went to the United States to seek refuge, but his sense of moral courage made him return to Germany two weeks later, writing,

"I will have no right to participate in the reconstruction of Christian life in Germany after the war if I do not share the trials of this time with my people." The next year Bonhoeffer charged that "the Church was silent when it should have cried out because the blood of the innocent was crying aloud to heaven. She is guilty of the deaths of the weakest and most defenceless brothers of Jesus Christ."[11]

Bonhoeffer and a friend personally helped some Jews move to neutral Switzerland, most probably saving their lives. Although his views of international affairs were near pacifism, and his Christian faith caused him to struggle with the decision, he nonetheless became involved in a plot to overthrow Adolf Hitler which led to Bonhoeffer's imprisonment and execution by hanging on Sunday, April 8, 1945. On April 30, just a few weeks later, Hitler committed suicide and Germany surrendered on May 8, 1945.

H. Fischer-Hullstrung was the doctor at the prison camp where Bonhoeffer breathed his last. His account follows:

> On the morning of that day between five and six o'clock the prisoners were taken from their cells, and the verdicts of the court martial read out to them. Through the half-open door in one room of the huts I saw Pastor Bonhoeffer, before taking off his prison garb, kneeling on the floor praying fervently to his God. I was most deeply moved by the way this lovable man prayed, so devout and so certain that God heard his prayer. At the place of execution, he again said a short prayer and then climbed the steps to the gallows, brave and composed. His death ensued after a few seconds. In the almost fifty years that I worked as a doctor, I have hardly ever seen a man die so entirely submissive to the will of God.[12]

***

Corrie ten Boom and her family lived in Holland when the country surrendered to the Nazis. Her story is told in *The Hiding Place,* a book that exposes the evil of Hitler's war on the Jewish people. Corrie's father was a devoted Christian who offered his heart, home, and life to save hundreds of Jews from death.

They lived in a quiet, friendly community of Jews and Christians. Corrie's father had a small watchmaking and repair shop where everyone was welcome, not only to purchase but also to hear the Word of God. At eighty-two years of age, and after two years of Nazi occupation of Holland, Casper ten Boom offered hope in times of terrible evil. More and more Jews sought refuge in the home above the shop, as the wave of brutality swept over the country. The ten Boom family welcomed them, considering them "God's ancient people."

Because the ten Booms were strong and courageous in their faith in God, they became part of the underground dedicated to saving as many Jews as possible. But not without wondering, "Was this what God wanted in times like these? How should a Christian act when evil was in power?"[13] One day a man arrived who "Years later I would learn that he was one of the most famous architects in Europe, I knew him only as Mr. Smit."[14] He had heard of their efforts and he inspected their home for making a safe place. He noticed the many important and treasured books of Jewish theology brought for safekeeping by the rabbi of Haarlem, saying, "Just in case I should not be able to care for them...ah...indefinitely. Books do not age as you and I do, old friend. They will speak when we are gone, to generations we will never see. The books must survive."[15]

Finally Mr. Smit said, "This is where the false wall will go!" Over the next few days, workmen came and went very discreetly so as not to alert the many uniformed soldiers with guns who roamed the streets. When finished, the narrow room could hold several Jews and their belongings. Mr. Smit said of the room behind a cabinet of bookshelves, "The Gestapo could search for a year. They'll never find this one."[16]

One of the underground leaders came to inspect the room and told Corrie,

A raid may come any day. I don't see how you can avoid one. Scores of people in and out—and an NSB agent living up the street. Your secret room is no good to you if people can't get to it in time. I know this Leendert. He's a very passable electrician. Get him to put a buzzer in every room with a door or window on the street. Then hold practice drills until your people can disappear in that room without a trace in less than a minute.[17]

The hiding place as well as the network of "safe houses" that Corrie oversaw served to save the lives of about 800 Jews before the ten Boom family was betrayed by a neighbor and the family was sent to prison. Never losing their faith, they faced unconscionable circumstances including the death of Corrie's father in the Scheveningen prison.

Corrie and her sister Betsie were sent to Ravensbruck, known as the death camp, for the terrors inflicted upon the prisoners there. Jammed into a train boxcar that could hold about thirty people standing, more than eighty women were shoved into the car. Corrie had smuggled in a small Bible that miraculously wasn't discovered, "Dear God, you have given us this precious Book. You have kept it hidden through checkpoints and inspections, You have used it for so many…"

So when we were herded into that room ten minutes later, we were not poor, but rich. Rich in this new evidence of the care of Him who was God even of Ravensbruck. We stood beneath the spigots as long as the flow of icy water lasted, feeling it soften our lice-eaten skin. … Betsie and I arrived in Barracks 8, bringing not only the Bible, but a new knowledge of the power of God. There were three women already asleep in the bed assigned to us. They made room for us as best they could, but the mattress sloped and I kept sliding to the floor.

…Life grew harder. There was too much misery, too much suffering. Every day something grew too heavy. Will You carry this, Lord Jesus? But as the rest of the world grew stranger, one thing became increasingly clear. And that was the reason the two of us were here. From morning until lights-out, whenever we were not in ranks for roll call, our Bible was the center of an ever-widening circle of help and hope. We gathered around it, holding out our hearts to its warmth and light. The blacker the night around us grew, the brighter and truer burned the Word of God. "Who shall separate us from the love of Christ? Shall tribulation, or distress, or persecution, or famine, or nakedness, or peril, or sword? ... Nay, in all these things we are more than conquerors through him that loved us."

I would look about as Betsie read, watching the light leap from face to face. More than conquerors... It was a fact.[18]

The sisters were moved to another barrack that was designed to hold 400 women; there were 1,400 living there. The odor of the filthy dirty, rotten straw mattresses was overwhelming—as were the fleas that bit at every area of flesh exposed beyond the thin cotton dress the women were issued.

"Betsie, how can we live in such a place?" I wailed.

"Show us how." It was said so matter of factly it took me a second to realize she was praying. The distinction between prayer and the rest of life seemed to be vanishing for Betsie.

"Corrie!" she said excitedly. "In the Bible this morning. Where was it? Read that part again!"

I glanced down the long dim aisle to make sure no guard was in sight, then drew the bible from its pouch. "It was in First Thessalonians," I said. "Here it is: 'Comfort the frightened, help the weak, be patient with everyone. See that none of you repays evil for evil, but always seek to do good to one another and to all....'"

..."'Give thanks in *all* circumstances,'" Betsie quoted. "Fleas are part of this place where God has put us."

So we gave thanks for fleas.[19]

Because of the fleas no guards ever came near that barrack and the sisters had time to read the Bible and talk of God's love. There were so many women yearning to hear God's Word that they had to hold a second service after the evening roll call. Betsie's health got worse and worse and although the vitamin bottle miraculously continued to supply drops daily, Betsie died and her body was tossed onto the pile in the back of the so-called hospital. Twelve days later, Corrie was released from prison for unknown reasons.

But the reasons became very clear—Corrie ten Boom set up rehabilitation centers in the Netherlands and then worldwide to help heal the spiritual wounds of concentration camp survivors.

***

William Wilberforce was more than a local hero—he led the British campaign against slavery, changing the world's entire mindset regarding the tragedy of selling humans. After almost thirty years of relentlessly pursuing his quest to stop slavery in the British Empire, with victory in sight, he wrote not of his own pursuits but those of his God:

> Never surely had I more cause for gratitude than now, when carrying the great object of my life, to which a gracious Providence directed my thoughts twenty-six or twenty-seven years ago, and led my endeavours in 1787 or 1788. O Lord, let me praise Thee with my whole heart: for never surely was there any one so deeply indebted as myself; which way soever I look I am crowded with blessings. Oh may my gratitude be in some degree proportionate.[20]

Wilberforce died in the same year that an act was passed giving freedom to all slaves in the British Empire. The following tribute was written about him— may we as well wear a mantle as profoundly grounded in God "through the merits of Jesus Christ."

To the memory of William Wilberforce

... In an age and country fertile in great and good men,

He was among the foremost of those who
fixed the character of their times
Because to high and various talents
To warm benevolence and to universal
candour,
He added the abiding eloquence of a
Christian life.

Eminent as he was in every department of
public labour,
And a leader in every work of charity,
Whether to relieve the temporal or the
spiritual wants of his fellow men
His name will ever be specially identified
With those exertions
Which, by the blessing of God, removed
from England
The guilt of the African slave trade,
And prepared the way for the abolition of
slavery
In every colony of the empire.

In the prosecution of these objects,
He relied, not in vain, on God;
But in the progress, he was called to
endure
Great obloquy and great opposition:
He outlived, however, all enmity:
And, in the evening of his days,

Withdrew from public life and public
observation
To the bosom of his family.
Yet he died not unnoticed or forgotten by
his country:
The peers and commons of England,
With the Lord Chancellor, and the Speaker,
at their head,
Carried him to his fitting place
Among the mighty dead around,
Here to repose:
Till, through the merits of Jesus Christ,
His only Redeemer and Saviour,
(Whom, in his life and in his writings he had
desired to glorify,)
He shall rise in the resurrection of the
just.[21]

***

In the United States, **President Abraham Lincoln**
brought about the emancipation of the slaves after a
bloody civil war. From humble beginnings, Lincoln tried
and failed several times to become a legislator. His
diligence was fruitful and he became the 16th president
and realized the importance of God's presence in his
life, saying in 1862, "In the present civil war, it is quite
possible that God's purpose is something different
from the purpose of either party—and yet the human

instrumentalities, working just as they do, are of the best adaptation to effect His purpose." During the Civil War, Lincoln issued a preliminary Emancipation Proclamation, declaring that as of January 1, 1863, all slaves in the rebellious states "shall be then, thenceforward, and forever free." While this proclamation did not set slaves free, it was an important turning point in the war, transforming the fight to preserve the nation into a battle for human freedom.[22]

Martin Luther King Jr. was a Baptist minister who led the Civil Rights Movement in the United States 1950s until his death by assassination in 1968. He advocated equal rights for African Americans through peaceful protests. At that time, segregation meant that African Americans were legally or socially separated regarding housing, medical care, education, employment, military, and transportation. King stood up for those who had no voice, and in his famous "I Have a Dream" speech he said, in part:

> I have a dream that one day that one day
> this nation will rise up and live out the true
> meaning of its creed: "We hold these
> truths to be self-evident, that *all* men are
> created equal."
> I have a dream that one day my four little
> children will one day live in a nation where

they will not be judged by the color of their skin but by the content of their character. And when this happens, and when we allow freedom ring, when we let it ring from every village and every hamlet, from every state and every city, we will be able to speed up that day when *all* of God's children, black men and white men, Jews and Gentiles, Protestants and Catholics, will be able to join hands and sing the words of the old Negro spiritual: *Free at last! Free at last! Thank God Almighty, we are free at last!*[23]

***

William and Catherine Booth were Christians in London, England, in the 1800s dedicated to helping the poor, homeless, hungry, and destitute to hear the gospel of Jesus Christ. Their mantle of service to God was handed down to their son, and their daughter was the first female general to lead the organization. From then on, the mantle has been handed down to millions worldwide who work and volunteer at The Salvation Army. From providing shelter for homeless families to feeding hundreds of thousands in the hunger relief program to prison ministries, elderly services, and combating human trafficking, The Salvation Army's Christian foundation is on the front lines of battling the ills of our world. The Salvation Army's faith statement follows:

> The Salvation Army is a Christian organisation and part of the universal Christian Church. Its message and the lifestyle it advocates are based on the Bible's teaching. Its work is to make known the good news about Jesus Christ and to persuade people to become his followers. Everything The Salvation Army does is rooted in the faith of its members. The confidence Salvationists have in a loving and caring God finds outward expression in their love for humanity and their practical response to human need.[24]

There are many, many others who have passed on their mantles to the next generation that could be mentioned but these are a few notables who changed the world for the better. May it be said of us that we have changed our worlds for the better as well. Be it at the workplace, in the church, or at home, we have the God-given abilities, talents, and skills to make a positive difference.

Prayer

Heavenly Father, we praise You and thank You for Your mantle of protection that covers Your children.

We pray that our spiritual mantles will reveal to others Your goodness and graciousness—that we will wear them with humble pride and for Your glory. Almighty God, let it not be said of us that we are covered with our "own disgrace as with a mantle" (Psalm 109:29). Rather, may it be said of us that our mantles reflect You and all that is righteous. In Jesus' precious name, amen.

Chapter 8
The Tallit: Little Tent

The word tallit is often translated as "little tent." This is, however, incorrect, as *tal* means "dew"[1] and the Hebrew word for "little" is *qatan*.[2]

Therefore a literal interpretation of tallit as "little tent" is inappropriate. Nonetheless, from an etymological viewpoint, we can still accept this phrase. In Mishnaic Hebrew, the word tallit means "to cover," from the Hebrew *tillel* (to cover); from the Aramaic *tallel*, also meaning "to cover," and from the word *telal*, meaning "shade," which has Semitic roots.[3]

Taking the uniqueness of this language into consideration, we can see that over the centuries the practice of wearing the tallit has become widely accepted in most Jewish circles as symbolic of the wearer being enclosed in a personal little tent. The Tent of Meeting or Tabernacle, as it was also known, could not accommodate over six million Jews at any one time. Therefore, the tallit served as their own private sanctuary where they could meet with God.

Your tallit can be your prayer closet!

Back in those days, each man had his own prayer shawl, or tallit. He would pull his tallit over his head, forming a tent, where he would chant and sing Hebrew songs and call upon God. It was an intimate, private place, set apart from anyone else, enabling the man to totally focus upon God. Their tallitot were their prayer closets!

It is often said that when Balaam blessed Israel, he looked out from the mountain and saw God's people resting in their tents and in their tallitot and was moved to speak prophetically.

> By now Balaam realized that the Lord was determined to bless Israel, so he did not resort to divination as before. Instead, he turned and looked out toward the wilderness, where **he saw the people of Israel** camped, tribe by tribe. Then the Spirit of God came upon him, and this is the message he delivered: "This is the message of Balaam son of Beor, the message of the man whose eyes see clearly, the message of one who hears the words of God, who sees a vision from the Almighty, who bows down with eyes wide open: **How beautiful are your tents, O Jacob; how lovely are your homes, O Israel!** (Numbers 24:1-5)

Scholars also comment on the occupation of the apostle Paul *(Sha'ul)*, who was a Jewish Pharisee and also a tentmaker. As the tzitzit are usually tied under the supervision of a rabbi, many believe that he made tallitot, tents for prayer and not tents to live in.[4]

Tents and Blue

The Tent of Meeting or Tabernacle was built with precise specifications from God. Not surprisingly, He said to decorate the curtains with blue, purple, and scarlet thread, with loops of blue—almost the same description given for the tzitzit on the tallit.

> *Make the Tabernacle from ten curtains of finely woven linen. Decorate the curtains with **blue**, purple, and scarlet thread and with skillfully embroidered cherubim. These ten curtains must all be exactly the same size—42 feet long and 6 feet wide. Join five of these curtains together to make one long curtain, then join the other five into a second long curtain. Put **loops of blue** yarn along the edge of the last curtain in each set. The fifty loops along the edge of one curtain are to match the fifty loops along the edge of the other curtain. Then make fifty gold clasps and fasten the long curtains together with the clasps. In this way, the*

> Tabernacle will be made of **one continuous piece**
> (Exodus 26:1-5).

> *Make another curtain for the entrance to* **the sacred tent.** *Make it of finely woven linen and embroider it with exquisite designs, using* **blue,** *purple, and scarlet thread* (Exodus 26:36).

We discussed the color blue in Chapter 3 at great length, and now we see its inclusion as part of the grandeur and opulence of the sacred tent's multiple curtains. Also, as with the tallit, the curtains were to be made of one continuous piece, woven with no seams. God's plans are always faultless. All that He does and says and thinks is intertwined for the perfect outcome. All He asks of us is obedience—when we obey, His plans are carried out with precision. When we don't obey, life gets complicated very quickly, as our ways and wills are not faultless, rather they are most often selfish and self-aggrandizing.

> *I, the Lord, will punish the world for its evil and the wicked for their sin. I will crush the arrogance of the proud and humble the pride of the mighty* (Isaiah 13:11).

Finding our own "little tent" where we can be alone with God and focus on Him and His voice will prevent us from complicating His plans for us. When we meditate on His Word and kick out all other thoughts, we will be refreshed and ready to follow Him.

When the atarah (collar) of the tallit is held above a person's head, it forms a little tent—a little tabernacle. Back in biblical days, as the individual meditated, prayed, and chanted, often the person's arms would be held up and to the side, giving the tallit the appearance of having wings. The "wings of the tallit" are discussed in the next chapter.

Tent Meetings

Mentioned briefly in the previous chapter were William and Catherine Booth, cofounders of The Salvation Army. In his early pastorate days, William Booth became disillusioned with the traditional church and chose instead to travel throughout the country preaching. By invitation, in 1865, he set up a tent in a Quaker graveyard and held a series of evangelistic meetings in the East End of London. Before long, his tent was full of people eager to hear from the man who preached hope to anyone who would listen, including thieves, prostitutes, gamblers, and drunkards.

> In 1867, Booth had only 10 full-time workers, but by 1974, the number had grown to 1,000 volunteers and 42 evangelists.... They launched

an offensive throughout the British Isles, in some cases facing real battles as organized gangs mocked and attacked them. In spite of violence and persecution, some 250,000 people were converted under the ministry of The Salvation Army between 1881 and 1885.[5]

In the year 2016, The Salvation Army provided more than 60 million meals worldwide and more than 10 million nights of shelter for individuals and families. Catherine Booth preached under the tent as well. She believed that "Christians must be passionate about their faith, that if we are indifferent we can lose the capacity for love and service. She wrote, 'He doesn't ask you to go to chapel or join the church and pray but to get down and give your heart to Him, to choose whom you will serve, and do it at once, and everything else will follow.'"[6]

Worldwide evangelist Billy Graham first became known in 1949—under a tent as he preached in Los Angeles. Since then he has preached the gospel of Jesus Christ to nearly 215 million in more than 185 countries. Hundreds of millions more people have been reached through television, video, film, and webcasts. But it all started under a tent. That crusade in Los Angeles was scheduled for three weeks but because of the crowds that overflowed the full tent, it was extended to more than eight weeks. Likewise, one of his early crusades in London had to be expanded; it lasted twelve weeks. Graham received recognition from many political dignitaries worldwide and was also recognized by the Anti-Defamation league of the B'nai B'rith in 1968 and the National Conference of Christians and Jews in 1971 for his efforts to foster a better understanding among all faiths.[7]

In the 1700s, John and Charles Wesley and George Whitefield birthed the Methodist church while evangelizing "outdoors," something unheard of at the time. That denomination today claims more than 11 million members worldwide.[8] For one hundred years England went through a spiritual revival—as the result of having collapsed "to a degree that was never known in any Christian country," said Bishop Berkeley. Thomas Carlyle described the country's condition as "Stomach well alive, soul extinct." The people were caught up in evil—drunkenness, gambling, children dying in workhouses, the slave trade, and public executions as entertainment. Sir William Blackstone visited the church of every major clergyman in London, but "did not hear a single discourse which had more Christianity in it than the writings of Cicero."[9]

> About the same time, George Whitefield, an ordained Anglican clergyman, was converted and in 1737 began preaching in London and Bristol. In order to reach the many non-church-goers, Whitefield spoke in the open fields, and large crowds began gathering to hear the message of

salvation. Whitefield became an itinerant preacher, or "one of God's runabouts," as he called himself, traveling extensively in his wide-ranging ministry. In his day, itinerant preachers were often criticized as interfering with or undermining the role of the parish priest. Whitefield countered that many of the established clergy could not bring life to their people since they themselves were spiritually dead.[10]

In the United States today, "Tent Revivals" are generally associated with Protestant churches hoping to revitalize their congregations. In earlier times in the US, tent preaching was known for featuring healing evangelists including: John G. Lake, Smith Wigglesworth, Kathryn Kuhlman, William Joseph Seymour, Aimee Semple McPherson, Oral Roberts, and Jack Coe just to name a few. They professed hundreds of miracle healings over the years of 1947-1958. Many of these pastors are controversial and their tactics and outcomes questioned, but God uses people in ways only He understands at times. In our most modern age of mass communication, truth is many times hard to find. The Internet boasts of this and that, with nary a shred of credible evidence proving or disproving statements.

Indoor/Outdoor Tents

Today's camping tents keep outdoor adventurers safe from inclement weather, stinging insects, and biting small animals. Most tents, though, are not sturdy enough to prevent large beasts, torrential downpours, or long-term freezing temperatures that would harm the campers. As we consider a tallit as a little tent, we can surmise that while holding the tallit above our heads, or even if we allow them to rest atop our heads, we can become encased and protected in a type of cocoon. Although not totally enveloped by the tallit, we can feel safe, secure, and comforted knowing that we are surrounded by Him as we reach out in prayer.

Our study of the tallit as a little tent cannot close without examining 2 Corinthians 5:1:

> *For we know that when **this earthly tent** we live in is taken down (that is, when we die and leave this earthly body), we will have a house in heaven, an eternal body made for us by God himself and not by human hands.*

I like The Message version of 2 Corinthians 5:1-5 that says:

> *For instance, we know that **when these bodies of ours are taken down like tents** and folded away, they will be replaced by resurrection bodies in heaven—God-made, not handmade—and **we'll never have to relocate our "tents" again.***

*Sometimes we can hardly wait to move—and so we cry out in frustration. Compared to what's coming, living conditions around here seem like a stopover in an unfurnished shack, and we're tired of it! We've been given a glimpse of the real thing, our true home, our resurrection bodies! The Spirit of God whets our appetite by giving us a taste of what's ahead. **He puts a little of heaven in our hearts so that we'll never settle for less.***

Just as tallitot are made by human hands and deteriorate, so our human bodies are deteriorating daily. The older we get the more aches and pains we have. Our bodies change in a variety of ways, most of the ways are not pleasant when over a certain age. Yet our eternal body is made for us by God himself—it will never wear out, be broken or diseased, or suffer injury. Oh what a glorious day it will be when we put on our resurrected bodies.

*and he has identified us as his own by **placing the Holy Spirit in our hearts** as the first installment that guarantees everything he has promised us* (2 Corinthians 1:22).

While we are on earth, though, we must revere our bodies as God's temple that house the Holy Spirit. Likewise, if we choose to wear a tallit, a little tent, while praying, we must do so with reverence and respect. This time with God can be another place, another prayer closet where you can commune with your heavenly Father—heart to heart.

> *But when you pray, go away by yourself, shut the door behind you, and **pray to your Father in private**. Then your Father, who sees everything, will reward you* (Matthew 6:6).

I've heard it said that some people consider their prayer closets as a "supply closet." They go to God with a list of wants and expect Him to dole out whatever they think they need. This is not the right attitude with which to approach God. First of all, He deserves our praise, worship, and thanksgiving when we enter our prayer closet or put on our tallit. Then He merits a period of quiet when He can search our hearts and spirits. Next we must seek His Kingdom—and then all we desire will be added unto us! (Matthew 6:33).

Seeking His Kingdom means shoving aside our selfish desires and ego-driven wants. Serving the King of kings means being subject to His will and ways, which are always perfect. Bowing to His plans for our lives means knowing that we will never have to worry about paying the bills, finding a job, mending relationships, being joyful and having peace. For all those things and *everything* is entrusted into His anything-is-possible hands.

Jesus told His disciples:

> **In this manner,** *therefore,* **pray:** *Our Father in heaven, hallowed be Your name. Your kingdom come. Your will be done on earth as it is in heaven. Give us this day our daily bread. And forgive us our debts, as we forgive our debtors. And do not lead us into temptation, but deliver us from the evil one. For Yours is the kingdom and the power and the glory forever. Amen* (Matthew 6:9-13).

There have been thousands of sermons preached on "The Lord's Prayer" and I'm sure you may have heard many. Yet there are nuances in the Matthew Henry Commentary that are important to share with you. Portions of the commentary follow:

> So many were the corruptions that had crept into this duty of prayer among the Jews, that Christ saw it needful to give a new directory for prayer, to show his disciples what must ordinarily be the matter and method of their prayer, which he gives in words that may very well be used as a form; as the summary or contents of the several particulars of our prayers.
>
> Not that we are tied up to the use of this form only, or of this always, as if this were necessary to the consecrating of our other prayers; we are here bid to pray after this manner, with these words, or to this effect.

It is our Lord's prayer, it is of his composing, of his appointing; it is very compendious, yet very comprehensive, in compassion to our infirmities in praying. The matter is choice and necessary, the method instructive, and the expression very concise. It has much in a little, and it is requisite that we acquaint ourselves with the sense and meaning of it, for it is used acceptably no further than it is used with understanding and without vain repetition. The Lord's prayer (as indeed every prayer) is a letter sent from earth to heaven. Here is the inscription of the letter, the person to whom it is directed, our Father; the where, in heaven; the contents of it in several errands of request; the close, for thine is the kingdom; the seal, Amen; and if you will, the date too, this day. Plainly thus: there are three parts of the prayer. I. The preface, Our Father who art in heaven. Before we come to our business, there must be a solemn address to him with whom our business lies; Our Father. Intimating, that we must pray, not only alone and for ourselves, but with and for others; for we are members one of another, and are called into fellowship with each other. We are here taught to whom to pray, to God only, and not to saints and angels, for they are ignorant of us, are not to have the high honours we give in prayer, nor can give favours we expect. We are taught how to address ourselves to God, and what title to give him, that which speaks him rather beneficent than magnificent, for we are to come boldly to the throne of grace.

II. The petitions, and those are six; the three first relating more immediately to God and his honour, the three last to our own concerns, both temporal and spiritual; as in the ten commandments, the four first teach us our duty toward God, and the last six our duty toward our neighbour. The method of this prayer teaches us to seek first the kingdom of God and his righteousness, and then to hope that other things shall be added.

1. Hallowed be thy name. It is the same word that in other places is translated sanctified. But here the old word hallowed is retained, only because people were used to it in the Lord's prayer.

2. Thy kingdom come. This petition has plainly a reference to the doctrine which Christ preached at this time, which John the Baptist had preached before, and which he afterwards sent his apostles out to preach—the kingdom of heaven is at hand. The kingdom of your Father who is in heaven, the kingdom of the Messiah, this is at hand, pray that it may come.

3. Thy will be done in earth as it is in heaven. We pray that God's kingdom being come, we and others may be brought into obedience to all the laws and ordinances of it. By this let it appear that Christ's kingdom is come, let God's will be done; and by this let is appear that it is come as a kingdom of heaven, let it introduce a heaven upon earth. We make Christ but a titular Prince, if we call him King, and do not do his will: having prayed that he may rule us, we pray that we may in every thing be ruled by him.

4. Give us this day our daily bread. Because our natural being is necessary to our spiritual well-being in this world, therefore, after the things of God's glory, kingdom, and will, we pray for the necessary supports and comforts of this present life, which are the gifts of God, and must be asked of him, Ton arton epiousion—Bread for the day approaching, for all the remainder of our lives. Bread for the time to come, or bread for our being and subsistence, that which is agreeable to our condition in the world (Prov. 30:8), food convenient for us and our families, according to our rank and station.

III. The conclusion: For thine is the kingdom, and the power and the glory, for ever. Amen. Some refer this to David's doxology, 1 Chr. 29:11. Thine, O Lord, is the greatness. It is,

1. A form of plea to enforce the foregoing petitions. It is our duty to plead with God in prayer, to fill our mouth with arguments (Job. 23:4) not to move God, but to affect ourselves; to encourage the faith, to excite our fervency, and to evidence both. Now the best pleas in prayer are those that are taken from God himself, and from that which he has made known of himself. We must wrestle with God in his own strength, both as to the nature of our pleas and the urging of them. The plea here has special reference to the first three petitions; "Father in heaven, thy kingdom come, for thine is the kingdom; thy will be done, for thine is the power; hallowed be thy name, for thine is the glory." And as to our own particular errands, these are encouraging: "Thine is the kingdom; thou hast the government of the world, and the protection of the saints, thy willing subjects in it;" God gives and saves like a king. "Thine is the power, to maintain and support that kingdom, and to make good all thine engagements to thy people." Thine is the glory, as the end of all that which is given to, and done for, the saints, in answer to their prayers; for their praise waiteth for him. This is a matter of comfort and holy confidence in prayer.

2. It is a form of praise and thanksgiving. The best pleading with God is praising of him; it is the way to obtain further mercy, as it qualifies us to receive it. In all our addresses to God, it is fit that praise should have a considerable share, for praise becometh the saints; they are to be our God for a name and for a praise. It is just and equal; we praise God, and give him glory, not because he needs it—he is praised by a world of angels, but because he deserves it; and it is our duty to give him glory, in compliance with his design in revealing himself to us. Praise is the work and happiness of heaven; and all that would go to heaven hereafter, must begin their heaven now. Observe, how full this doxology is, The kingdom, and the power, and the glory, it is all thine. Note, It becomes us to be copious in praising God. A true saint never thinks he can speak honourably enough of God: here there should be a gracious fluency, and this for ever. Ascribing glory to God for ever, intimates an acknowledgement, that it is eternally due, and an earnest desire to be eternally doing it, with angels and saints above, Ps. 71:14.

Lastly, To all this we are taught to affix our Amen, so be it. God's Amen is a grant; his fiat is, it shall be so; our Amen is only a summary desire; our fiat is, let it be so: it is in the token of our desire and assurance to be heard, that we say Amen. Amen refers to every petition going before, and thus, in compassion to our infirmities, we are taught to knit up the whole in one word, and so to gather up, in the general, what we have lost and let slip in the particulars. It is good to conclude religious duties with some warmth and vigour, that we may go from them with a sweet savour upon our spirits. It was of old the practice of good people to say, Amen, audibly at the end of every prayer, and it is a commendable practice, provided it be done with understanding, as the apostle directs (1 Co. 14:16), and uprightly, with life and liveliness, and inward expressions, answerable to that outward expression of desire and confidence.

Christ came into the world as the great Peace-Maker, and not only to reconcile us to God, but one to another, and in this we must comply with him. It is great presumption and of dangerous consequence, for any to make a light matter of that which Christ here lays such a stress upon. Men's passions shall not frustrate God's word.[11]

Dear friend, because your relationship with your heavenly Father is personal and unique—known only between the two of you, the words in this book are offered in love and as encouragement as you walk your own journey through life. It seems that the more we know about other Christians and other points of view, more of God is revealed to us. Not only is He alive in your heart and your spirit, He was alive and real in the hearts and spirits of all His children, from time eternal. Learning about their experiences and now shouldering their mantles brings His Kingdom and will on earth as it is in Heaven.

Prayer

Great High Priest, forgive us for being prideful and selfish in our prayers to You. Too often we focus on ourselves rather than You. You always have our best interests in mind, and in Your heart. Our desire to please You should be at the top of our priority list. Before we go to sleep at night, may we give You the praise You deserve. May we thank You for all the blessings of the day—for You provide us so very many every day. Upon awaking each morning, may we praise You for another day to give You glory in all that we do. In Jesus' name, amen and amen.

Chapter 9
The Tallit: The Wings

The four corners of a tallit with its fringes are also called the "wings" of the tallit. As the *atarah* is held above a person's head, it forms the wearer's own tent. The wings of the garment are formed when the arms of the wearer are held out.

In Numbers 15:38, the words "border" or "corner" is translated from the Old Testament Hebrew word *kanaf*, which can also mean "wings." For this reason, the corners of the prayer shawl are often called wings. The Hebrew word *kanaf* occurs in Psalm 91 where God's people are encouraged to "abide under the shadow of the Almighty" and also to trust in the protection given "under His wings."

> *Those who live in the shelter of the Most High will find rest in the shadow of the Almighty. This I declare about the Lord:* **He alone is my refuge, my place of safety; he is my God, and I trust him.** *For he will rescue you from every trap and protect you from deadly disease.* **He will cover you** *with his feathers.* **He will shelter you with his wings**

[kanaf]. *His faithful promises are your armor and protection* (Psalm 91:1-4).

In Ezekiel 16:4-8, the word "cloak" can also be translated "wing," which is the same Hebrew word used in Numbers 15. In Ezekiel 16, the Lord speaks to His people in an imagery passage saying:

> *On the day you were born, no one cared about you. Your umbilical cord was not cut, and you were never washed, rubbed with salt, and wrapped in cloth. No one had the slightest interest in you; no one pitied you or cared for you. On the day you were born, you were unwanted, dumped in a field and left to die. But I came by and saw you there, helplessly kicking about in your own blood. As you lay there, I said, "Live!" And I helped you to thrive like a plant in the field. You grew up and became a beautiful jewel. Your breasts became full, and your body hair grew, but you were still naked. And when I passed by again, I saw that you were old enough for love. So **I wrapped my cloak [kanaf] around you to cover** your nakedness and declared my marriage vows. I made a covenant with you, says the Sovereign Lord, and you became mine* (Ezekiel 16:4-8).

When we consider the interpretation of the cloak as wings, the significance of this passage of Scripture becomes clear. The Lord is speaking to His people, recounting that at the time they became a nation they were loathed and hated by all the heathen nations surrounding them. They were immature and polluted by their own sins, but He spoke a Word to His people, declaring that they should live.

Once that Word was spoken, the passage shows how God's people increased in number, wealth, and glory. We can see that, despite the condition of His people, God did not forsake them but looked on them in love.

Ezekiel 17 mentions the wings of the cherubim many times, and the study and discussion of this passage of Scripture could fill a book in itself—as could the mentions of wings in the book of Revelation.

Using the translation of the word "cloak" to wings, we can understand that when God speaks about spreading His cloak over His people, it can be interpreted as the Lord spreading His tallit over His people. The Lord makes it clear in this passage that His people have reached a place where they are ready for love and for commitment. Therefore, He spreads His tallit over them in the same way that a husband might spread his tallit over his bride during a Jewish wedding ceremony.

God's Promise

The Lord makes it clear that He is ready to make a promise to His people and to enter into covenant with them so that they truly become His people and He becomes their God. The act of entering into a covenant could then be seen to be represented by His cloak or wings—His tallit with the tzitzit—His commandments being accepted by His people as a statute forever.

Another phenomenon linked to the wings of the tallit is divine healing. As we look at key passages of Scripture, we find a significant link between the tallit and miraculous accounts of healing in the New Testament.

In various New Testament Scriptures, we can see where this translation of the fringes as wings become relevant. This translation is important when we consider the meaning of the word used for border or hem in the New Testament, which is the Greek word *kraspedon*, which is also translated fringe or tassel.[1]

> *Wherever he went—in villages, cities, or the countryside—they brought the sick out to the marketplaces. They begged him to let*

the sick touch at least the fringe of his robe, and *all who touched him were healed* (Mark 6:56).

When the people recognized Jesus, the news of his arrival spread quickly throughout the whole area, and soon people were bringing all their sick to be healed. They begged him to let the sick touch at least the fringe of his robe, and all who touched him were healed (Matthew 14:35-36).

In these accounts we find occasions where people were healed as they touched the hem or border (significantly the wings or fringes) of Jesus' garment. It is generally understood that Jesus, as an orthodox Jew, wore a tallit. Therefore, it is widely taught that it wasn't specifically the hem or border of the garment that people were reaching for but the tzitzit.

The story of the healing of one particular woman in the New Testament is told in three of the four Gospels (Matthew 9:20-22; Mark 5:25-34; Luke 8:43-48), giving us insight into several aspects of healing connected to the tzitzit, the wings. This event was discussed previously, but is worth repeating.

Just then a woman who had suffered for twelve years with constant bleeding came up behind him. **She touched the fringe of his robe, for she thought, "If I can just touch his robe, I will be healed."** Jesus turned around, and when he saw her he said, "Daughter, be encouraged! Your faith has made you well." And the woman was healed at that moment (Matthew 9:20-22).

A woman in the crowd had suffered for twelve years with constant bleeding, and she could find no cure. Coming up behind Jesus, **she touched the fringe of his robe. Immediately, the bleeding stopped.** "Who touched me?" Jesus asked. Everyone denied it, and Peter said, "Master, this whole crowd is pressing up against you." But Jesus said, **"Someone deliberately touched me, for I felt healing power go out from me."** When the woman realized that she could not stay hidden, she began to tremble and fell to her knees in front of him. The whole crowd heard her explain why **she had touched him and that she had been immediately healed.** "Daughter," he said to her, "your faith has made you well. Go in peace" (Luke 7:43-48).

Why would this woman stoop to touch the tzitzit, the wings of Jesus' garment? Why not reach out for His hands or His feet? It was clear that she had heard about Jesus and about the miracles that follow Him. Perhaps she realized that she didn't need to touch Him or need Him to touch her—all she needed was to touch His wings in faith, believing to be healed. Perhaps the Old Testament passage in Malachi became a reality to her in that moment. Before her very eyes, not far from her trembling grasp, stood the manifested embodiment of those ancient words:

> *But for you who fear my name, the Sun of Righteousness will rise with **healing in his wings.** And you will go free, leaping with joy like calves let out to pasture* (Malachi 4:2).

Just a few feet away from her faltering steps stood the Son of Righteousness, and she believed with all her heart that He had healing in His wings for her that day. Hallelujah!

> *Ruth fell at his feet and thanked him warmly. "What have I done to deserve such kindness?" she asked. "I am only a foreigner." "Yes, I know," Boaz replied. "But I also know about everything you have done for your mother-in-law since the death of your husband. I have heard how you left your father and mother and your own land*

*to live here among complete strangers. May the Lord, the **God of Israel, under whose wings you have come to take refuge,** reward you fully for what you have done"* (Ruth 2:10-12).

Not only does physical healing rise from His wings, but also family restoration. Ruth stayed with her mother-in-law even after her husband had died. Because of her faithfulness, she eventually became the wife of Boaz, perpetuating the family lineage, which includes Jesus. Ruth was the mother of Obed, the grandfather of King David. As we remain under His wings, we can take refuge in knowing that our future is secure.

In 2 Samuel 22, David sang a song of praise to the Lord after God had rescued him from all his enemies and from King Saul who sought to kill David. In the long and beautiful song, David mentions that His Savior was *"mounted on a mighty angelic being, he flew, soaring on the **wings of the wind"*** (2 Samuel 11). The praises coming from David are gripping—portraying the depth of his thankfulness and the power of his Lord.

On Eagles' Wings

Then Moses climbed the mountain to appear before God. The Lord called to him from the *mountain and said, "Give these instructions to the family of Jacob; announce it to the descendants of Israel: 'You have seen what I did to the Egyptians. You know how **I carried you on eagles' wings and brought you to myself.** Now if you will obey me and keep my covenant, you will be my own special treasure from among all the peoples on earth; for all the earth belongs to me. And you will be my kingdom of priests, my holy nation.' This is the message you must give to the people of Israel"* (Exodus 19:3-6).

In Exodus 19, God speaks to Moses, reminding him of how His Lord carried him and the people out of slavery and to Himself, into freedom and safety. God promises them that He will make them His "own special treasure" and a "kingdom of priests"—if they will obey Him and keep His covenant. God asks so little of us, yet we are so easily turned aside, tripping and falling off the path of righteousness.

Eagles are majestic creatures, it is no wonder that God uses this image to capture the imagination of Moses— and us—as the mighty Lord soars with His children above the chaos and fray of a world in turmoil. There He is carrying us across the blue skies, floating along with effortless ease.

When we think of wings, it evokes the sense of freedom. For example, looking up and seeing a bird of any kind, it seems the creature is enjoying the day, God's creation. We may think of flying away to a much-needed vacation. "On eagle's wings" or "in a beeline" are expressions for the shortest distance between two points. When we obey the Lord and keep His covenant, we don't have to wander in the wilderness for 40 years, we have a beeline to Him; our path is as the eagle flies into His throne room. There we can find shelter and security.

Two other verses in the Psalms beautifully depict the Lord's wings of safety:

> How precious is your unfailing love, O God! **All humanity finds shelter in the shadow of your wings** (Psalm 36:7).
> Let me live forever in your sanctuary, **safe beneath the shelter of your wings!** (Psalm 61:4).

Other verses come to mind when thinking of safety and our feathered friends:

> Like an eagle that rouses her chicks and hovers over her young, so **he spread his wings to take them up and carried them safely** on his pinions (Deuteronomy 32:11).

> O Jerusalem, Jerusalem, the city that kills the prophets and stones God's messengers!

*How often **I have wanted to gather your children together as a hen protects her chicks beneath her wings,** but you wouldn't let me* (Matthew 23:37).

How comforting it is to know we are protected, safe, and secure beneath the wings of Jesus the Lord and Savior. We are covered with His love, just as we are covered with the blood He shed on the cross for us. Psalm 85:2 says of God, "You forgave the guilt of your people—yes, you covered all their sins."

> *Most important of all, continue to show deep love for each other, for love covers a multitude of sins* (1 Peter 4:8).

A long-popular song by Michael Joncas, "On Eagle's Wings," [2] has a melody and words that stay in a person's mind and spirit long after the music stops:

> You who dwell in the shelter of the Lord,
> Who abide in His shadow for life,
> Say to the Lord, "My Refuge,
> My Rock in Whom I trust."

> And He will raise you up on eagle's wings,
> Bear you on the breath of dawn,
> Make you to shine like the sun,
> And hold you in the palm of His hand.

The snare of the fowler will never capture you,
And famine will bring you no fear;
Under His wings your refuge,
His faithfulness your shield.

You need not fear the terror of the night,
Nor the arrow that flies by day,
Though thousands fall about you,
Near you it shall not come.

For to His angels he's given a command,
To guard you in all of your ways,
Upon their hands they will bear you up,
Lest you dash your foot against a stone.

And He will raise you up on eagle's wings,
Bear you on the breath of dawn,
Make you to shine like the sun,
And hold you in the palm of His hand.

Prayer

Lord God, please cover us with Your wings of love that cover our sin and shame. Like the strong, swift eagle, may we fly to You in humble adoration and soaring praise for the God Almighty, the great I AM. Of all Your creation, the birds of the air are majestic wonders, gliding along on the wind, keeping an eye on life below. "But those who trust in the Lord will find new strength. They will soar high on wings like eagles. They will run and not grow weary. They will walk and not faint (Isaiah 40:31). May this be us, heavenly Father—trusting in You and finding new strength daily as we serve You. In Jesus' name we pray, amen.

A Final Note

With the growing popularity of the tallit among Christians, it is generally said that Christians should not or are not obliged to wear a tallit or embrace its spiritual truths, as the laws regarding it were only given to the Jewish nation, not to the Gentiles.

Whereas it is true that Christians are not obliged to adhere to many of the laws prevalent in the Jewish way of life, the merits of many Jewish customs become significant when considering the events portrayed in the Bible in their original context. Therefore, it is not surprising that Christians are drawn to many of these practices, as they have their roots in the Bible, the Holy Word of God.

Accepting for themselves the promises of the New Testament, Christians everywhere can enjoy and benefit from this sacred rite.

> *For all who are led by the Spirit of God are children of God. So you have not received a spirit that makes you fearful slaves. Instead, **you received God's Spirit when he adopted you as his own children. Now we call him, "Abba, Father"*** (Romans 8:14-15).

*So the promise is received by faith. It is given as a free gift. And we are all certain to receive it, whether or not we live according to the law of Moses, if we have faith like Abraham's. For **Abraham is the father of all who believe.** (Romans 4:16).*

*In the same way, "Abraham believed God, and God counted him as righteous because of his faith." **The real children of Abraham, then, are those who put their faith in God.** What's more, the Scriptures looked forward to this time when **God would make the Gentiles right in his sight because of their faith.** God proclaimed this good news to Abraham long ago when he said, "All nations will be blessed through you"* (Galatians 3:6-8).

*But Christ has rescued us from the curse pronounced by the law. When he was hung on the cross, he took upon himself the curse for our wrongdoing. For it is written in the Scriptures, "Cursed is everyone who is hung on a tree." **Through Christ Jesus, God has blessed the Gentiles with the same blessing he promised to Abraham, so that we who are believers might receive the promised Holy Spirit through faith*** (Galatians 3:13-14).

Christians can enjoy special times of prayer using a tallit. It is amazing that so much symbolism could be encompassed in one piece of cloth. The tallit serves as an eternal reminder of God's commandments, His constant love for His people, His promises, His divine protection, and His healing power.

If you choose to wear a tallit when you pray, may you recall that this action is symbolic of being wrapped up in God's Word—in His loving arms. I pray that the divine presence of the Holy Spirit will be more real to you each time you pray in your own "little tent"; and each time you look at the tzitzit, may you remember God's Word and obey it. Remember that the God you serve has healing in His wings.

Endnotes

Chapter 1 – The Tallit: The Word

1. Strong's Exhaustive Concordance, s.v. "talitha (5008)" taleh (2924)," and "tela (2922)" (Grand Rapids, MI: Associated Publishers and Authors, Inc.).

2. Gary Collet and Debra Collet, "Talit: The Jewish Prayer Shawl," Jews 4 Jesus. http://www.jews4jesus.co.uk/scripture/talit_shawl .html; accessed October 8, 2007.

3. John D. Garr, *The Hem of His Garment: Touching the Power in God's Word* (Atlanta, GA: Golden Key Press, 2007).

4. Ibid.

Chapter 2 – What Is a Tallit?

1. Jewish book of the Law; the first five books of the Hebrew Scriptures: Genesis, Exodus, Leviticus, Numbers, and Deuteronomy. Hebrew words and phrases are used throughout the book as it is important to be familiar with God's children's language—we are, after all, all children of YHVH, siblings of Yeshua.

2. "A list of the 613 Mitzvot," *Judaism 101,* http://www.jewfaq.org/613.htm; accessed February 7, 2017.

3. Adam Barnett, "The Tales of the Tallit," *JustChristianNews.com*; http://www.articlesbase.com/religion-articles/the-tales-of-the-tallit-70679.html; accessed February 7, 2017.
4. Alden Oreck, "The Cairo Genizah," Jewish Virtual Library; http://www.jewishvirtuallibrary.org/the-cairo-genizah; accessed February 11, 2017.

Chapter 3 – What Are the Tzitzit?
1. Strong's Exhaustive Concordance, s.v. "teklet (8504)."
2. Levi bar Ido, "Why the Hassle over Tassles?"; https://www.scribd.com/document/2641825/tassels; accessed February 11, 2017.
3. Ibid.
4. Mois A. Navon, "Historical Review of Tekhelet and the Hillazon," *Ptil Tekhelet*; http://www.tekhelet.com/timeline.htm; accessed February 11, 2017.
5. Ellie Zolfagharifard, "Sacred blue snail dye seen only twice since Jesus was alive is discovered on Israeli cloth," January 2, 2014, Dailymail.co.uk; http://www.dailymail.co.uk/sciencetech/article-2532623/Sacred-blue-snail-dye-seen-twice-Jesus-alive-discovered-Israeli-cloth.html; accessed February 10, 2017.

6. "Macrame," *Target Woman,*
http://www.targetwoman.com/articles/macrame.
html; accessed October 8, 2007.
7. "Tallit Talk," Rabbi
Scheinerman.net/Judaism/tallit/; accessed
February 11, 2017.
8. Ibid.

Chapter 4 – What Is the Atarah?
1. Arba Kanfot, "Wearing the Tallit Katan,"
Hebrew for Christians,
http://www.hebrew4christians.com/Blessings/Dail
y_Blessings/Tallit_Katan/tallit_katan.html;
accessed February 11, 2017.
2. The Three Arches Co., Ltd., "The New Covenant
Prayer Shawl";
https://www.holylandshopping.com/search?contr
oller=search&orderby=position&orderway=desc&
search_query=prayer+shawl&submit_search=;
accessed February 11, 2017.

Chapter 5 – Wearing a Tallit
1. "Bar Mitzvah, Bat Mitzvah and Confirmation,"
Judaism 101, http// www.jewfaq.org/barmitz.htm;
accessed February 11, 2017.
2. "Kol Nidrei," Jewish Enclyclopedia;
http://www.iyyun.com.holidays/YomKippur/Kol%2
0Nidrei.html; accessed February 11, 2017.

3. "Simchat Torah," Hebrew for Christians; http://www.hebrew4christians.com/Holidays/Fall_ Holidays/Simchat_Torah/simchat_torah.html; accessed February 11, 2017.

4. Strong's Exhaustive Concordance, s.v. "phylactery (5440)."

5. Bradford Richardson, "Reaction to Trump preferred refugee status reveals 'blind spot' to Christian persecution," *The Washington Times,* February 9, 2017; http://www.washingtontimes.com/news/2017/feb/ 9/negative-reaction-to-trump-preferred-refugee-statu/; accessed February 10, 2017.

6. Stephen Oryszczuk, "Anti-Semitism at highest level on record," *Times of Israel,* February 2, 2017; http://jewishnews.timesofisrael.com/cst-report-2016/; accessed February 10, 2017.

7. "Global Anti-Semitism: Selected Incidents Around the World in 2014," Andi-Defamation League, December 31, 2014; http://www.adl.org/anti-semitism/international/c/global-antisemitism-2014.html; accessed February 10, 2017.

Chapter 6 – The Tallit: The Covering

1. Rabbi Mordechai Becher, "The Jewish Wedding Ceremony," http://ohr.edu/1087; accessed February 10, 2017.

2. "What happens during a Jewish wedding?" Usenet FAQ, http://www.faqs.org/faqs/judaism/FAQ/04-Observance/section-65.html (accessed February 10, 2017).

3. Rabbi Adin Steinsaltz, "Kippot, Hats and Head Coverings: A Traditionalist View," Reprinted with permission from *Teshuvah: A Guide for the Newly Observant Jew* (Jason Aronson); MyJewishLearning; http://www.myjewishlearning.com/article/kippot-hats-and-head-coverings-a-traditionalist-view/; accessed February 11, 2017.

Chapter 7 – The Tallit: The Mantle

1. Yahchannah Wolf, "Do not study Torah, Gentile!" Liberty Mountain of YHWH is TRUE Liberty and Life; http://www.qumran.com/do_not_study_torah_gentile.htm; accessed February 11, 2017.

2. "Torah Readings," Judaism 101; http://www.jewfaq.org/readings.htm; accessed February 11, 2017.

3. Torah Ornaments, Jewish Virtual Library; http://www.jewishvirtuallibrary.org/torah-ornaments; accessed February 11, 2017.

4. "Torah Mantles," Harwin Studios; http://www.harwinstudios.com/commissions/torah.php; accessed February 11, 2017.

5. D. James Kennedy, "Was Alabama Judge Roy Moore wrong for not obeying a federal court order to remove a monument to the Ten Commandments?" ChristianAnswers.net; November 4, 2003; http://christiananswers.net/q-eden/judgemoore.html; accessed February 12, 2017.

6. "Ten Commandments judge removed from office," CNN.com, November 14, 2003; http://www.cnn.com/2003/LAW/11/13/moore.tenco mmandments/; accessed February 12, 2017.

7. Ibid.

8. Beatrice Gitau, "Oklahoma Ten Commandments monument ordered to be removed," *The Christian Science Monitor,* June 30, 2015; http://www.csmonitor.com/USA/USA-Update/2015/0630/Oklahoma-Ten-Commandments-monument-ordered-to-be-removed-video; accessed February 14, 2017.

9. Cathy Burke, "Franklin Graham: 'Everything Related to God' Is Under Attack," Newsmax.com, July 3, 2015; http://www.newsmax.com/Newsfront/franklin-graham-god-under-attack/2015/07/03/id/653409/; accessed February 12, 2017.

10. Eric Metaxas, *Bonhoeffer* (Nashville, TN: Nelson Books, 2014).

11. Franklin Sherman, "Dietrich Bonhoeffer," *Encyclopaedia Britannica,* October 11, 2016;

https://www.britannica.com/biography/Dietrich-Bonhoeffer; accessed February 12, 2017.

12. Metaxas, *Bonhoeffer*; Eberhard Bethge, *Dietrich Bonhoeffer, A Biography*, rev. ed. (Minneapolis: Augsburg Fortress, 2000), 927-28.

13. Corrie ten Boom, *The Hiding Place* (Bloomington, MN: Chosen Books, 1971 and 1984).

14. Ibid.

15. Ibid.

16. Ibid.

17. Ibid.

18. Ibid.

19. Ibid.

20. Eric Metaxas, *Amazing Grace* (New York: HarperCollins, 2007).

21. Ibid.

22. http://www.history.com/topics/american-civil-war/emancipation-proclamation; accessed February 13, 2017.

23. http://www.americanrhetoric.com/speeches/mlkihaveadream.htm; accessed February 13, 2017.

24. http://www.salvationarmy.org/ihq/faith; accessed February 13, 2017.

Chapter 8 – The Tallit: Little Tent

1. Strong's Exhaustive Concordance, s.v. "tal (2919)."

2. Strong's Exhaustive Concordance, s.v. "ith (6996)."

3. TheFreeDictionary.com, s.v. "tallis." http://www.thefreedictionary.com/tallis; accessed October 8, 2007.

4. "Little Tent, a Prayer Closet"; http://www.msgr.ca/msgr-8/Prayer_Shawls_2.htm; accessed February 11, 2017.

5. The Salvation Army; http://www.salvationarmyusa.org/usn/history-of-the-salvation-army; accessed February 13, 2017.

6. The Salvation Army; http://www.salvationarmyusa.org/usn/people#wbooth; accessed February 13, 2017.

7. Billy Graham; https://billygraham.org/about/biographies/billy-graham/; accessed February 13, 2017.

8. http://christianity.about.com/od/methodistdenomination/a/John-Wesley.htm; accessed February 13, 2017.

9. Diane Severance, "Evangelical Revival in England," Christianity.com; http://www.christianity.com/church/church-history/timeline/1701-1800/evangelical-revival-in-england-11630228.html; accessed February 14, 2017.

10. Ibid.

11. Matthew Henry Commentary on Matthew 6; http://www.biblestudytools.com/commentaries/matthew-henry-complete/matthew/6.html; accessed February 14, 2017.

Chapter 9 – The Tallit: The Wings
1. Strong's Exhaustive Concordance, s.v. "kraspedon (2899)."
2. Michael Joncas, "On Eagle's Wings," OCP label, 1977.

About the Author

Bishop John Francis challenges the Body of Christ to shake off complacency and live as God intended—fruitful and effective. He is uncompromising and means serious business for God. As a result, he is always in great demand for preaching engagements, as well as imparting ministerial advice and spiritual wisdom through the covering he offers pastors as part of his established Ruach Network of Churches.

Bishop John and Co-Pastor Penny Francis are the founders of the United Kingdom's premier Christian TV, "Flow TV," and launched their new station in March 2014, "Bringing Hope, Inspiring Change."

Operating in his gift as an apostle and speaking with a prophetic voice, Bishop Francis is the founder and senior pastor of Ruach City Church—one church in several locations (Brixton in South London; Kilburn in North London; Walthamstow in East London, Birmingham, UK, and Philadelphia in the United States). Ruach City Church is one of the largest and fastest growing churches in the UK. Starting from humble beginnings, with only eighteen faithful members, the church has grown rapidly and continues to grow. Several services are held every Sunday at several locations.

Bishop John Francis' outreach ministries are many, including his role as international director of the Ruach Network of Churches, overseeing approximately 50 churches in the UK and overseas. In 2012, Ruach City Church launched *Ruach Radio* via Internet (www.ruachradio.com) and can also be heard London-wide on DAB Radio.

A recipient of the British Gospel Association's Award, *Contribution to Gospel Music* and *Gospel TV Series of the Year* (as co-presenter of the UK's pioneering Gospel TV program, *People Get Ready!*), Bishop Francis is a multitalented, multifaceted man of God. He has performed in the presence of Her Majesty, the Queen, the Prince and late Princess of Wales, as well as toured throughout Europe presenting musical workshops and television and radio shows with the renowned Inspirational Choir (UK).

Bishop Francis was awarded the Minister of the Year Oasis Award and Church of the Year Oasis Award; and the Bishop Francis Choir—The Ruach

City Church Choir and Musicians recorded on the *Donnie McClurkin "Live in London" Album,* which has now reached platinum level sales—reaching multiple thousands of souls.

Bishop Francis is also the co-chair of Empowered 21 (E21) and a member of The Churches Together in England (CTE).

Bishop Francis' ministry is local, national, and international with more than 126 million viewers in the USA watching his broadcast ministry, *Order My Steps.* The Order My Steps Conference hosted its first international tour in Germany and Atlanta, USA, in 2004 and have held additional conferences in Jamaica and in the USA: Charlotte, North Carolina; Orlando, Florida; and Philadelphia, Pennsylvania.

Bishop Francis is the author of several outstanding books including: *Walking In Your Assignment, Is There a Word from the Lord?, What Do You Do When You're Left Alone?, 10 Steps to Get out of Debt, The Pastors & Church Workers Handbook,* and has released four CDs entitled *Finally, Bishop John Francis, One Lord, One Faith, Manifestation of the Promise,* and the most current, *Welcome in this Place.*

Bishop Francis's wife, Penny, is the Co-Pastor of Ruach City Church and has worked alongside him throughout his ministry. They have three lovely daughters, Juanita, Teleisa, and Charisa.

Ministry Contact Information

Website
www.johnfrancis.org.uk

Phone
Ruach City Church
+44 (020) 8678 6888

Email Bishop's Office
global@ruachcitychurch.org

Facebook: BishopJohnFrancis
Twitter: BishopJFrancis
Instagram: BishopJFrancis
Periscope: BishopJFrancis

PAPERBACKS AVAILABLE AT

www.johnfrancis.org.uk
AND ALL GOOD BOOKSTORES
EBOOK VERSIONS ALSO AVAILABLE ON APPLE® iBooks
AMAZON KINDLE

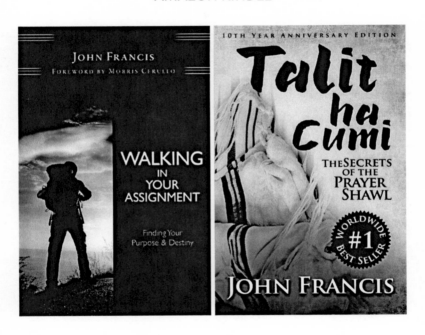

Notes

Notes

_____

_____

_____

_____

_____

_____

_____

_____

_____

Notes

Notes

Notes

_____

_____

_____

_____

_____

_____

_____

_____

_____